State-Of-The-Art Cohousing:
Lessons Learned from Quimper Village

Alexandria Levitt and Charles Durrett

with Quimper Village Residents

Cataloging in Publication Data:
A catalog record for this publication is available from Durrett Architects

**Copyright © 2020 by Alexandria Levitt & Charles Durrett.
All rights reserved.**

Cover design by Zishi Han
Cover photo: Quimper Village Life © Janet Palmer/Deja View Photography. All others courtesy of Charles Durrett and the residents of Quimper Village

Printed by Kindle Direct Publishing

Paperback ISBN: 978-0-945929-05-5

Library of Congress Number: 2019920320

Inquiries regarding requests to reprint all or part of
State-Of-The-Art Cohousing: Lessons Learned from Quimper Village
should be addressed to Durrett Architects at the address below

To order directly from the authors, please call 1-530-265-9980

Any other inquiries can be sent directly by mail to:

Durrett Architects
241 Commercial Steet. Unit B.
Nevada City, CA 95959

This book is dedicated to Pat Hundhausen, who, with vision and faith in her fellow citizens, set a community of elders up for long-term success.

Contents

Acknowledgments	xv
Foreword	xi
Introduction	1
Chapter 1 *Let's Talk*	6
Chapter 2 *The Getting-It-Built Workshop*	16
Chapter 3 *Be Part of the Dream*	24
Chapter 4 *Building a Community*	34
Chapter 5 *Professional Partnerships*	42
Chapter 6 *Dynamic What?*	52
Chapter 7 *Time Is Money*	58
Chapter 8 *Finding and Purchasing Six Acres*	68
Chapter 9 *The Design of Quimper Village*	76
Chapter 10 *Constructing Quimper Village*	90
Chapter 11 *Living There: Was It All Worth It?*	112
Appendix:	
A - *What they Did Right*	119
B - *Guidelines for Team Decisions*	123
C - *Inspirational Talk for General Meeting*	127
D - *Invitation to QV's Final Meeting*	129
E - *QV's Development Timeline*	133
Senior Cohousing Certification	139
About the Authors	143

Acknowledgments

This book would not have been possible without the wonderful residents of Quimper Village. In June 2018, they hosted a weekend long conference where they spoke at length about how they created their neighborhood. Those presentations became the inspiration and core of this book. We can't thank them enough for mustering up their heartfelt sentiments about living there.

We'd like to thank Zishi Han and Kim Stewart for putting their heart and soul into making this book beautiful. And thanks to Darren Chapel for coordinating and editing, and for being the all-around "make it happen" guy. For the editing, we'd like to thank Diane Durrett, Mike van Mantgem, and David Hundhausen for making our meaning clear. Your role in this process was invaluable.

And lastly, thank you to all the architects and designers/implementers from the MDA staff for manifesting the dream, the local architects for following through, the builder and project manager, and all of the consultants and lawyers who made Quimper Village a reality. And, of course, Kathryn McCamant, who personally guided them through rough seas and into port.

Foreword

By **Jill Vitale-Aussem**
President & CEO of The Eden Alternative

When I first met Chuck Durrett and experienced the intentional interdependence and community-building that occurs in cohousing, everything clicked into place. I had long been concerned that hospitality, resort-style living, and customer service had taken center stage in senior living–promising perfection, a pristine experience and carefree lifestyles.

Cohousing is different.

Cohousing isn't about moving a group of people into a communal living environment and putting a "community" sign out front. It's people exerting real influence on the shape of their living environment, working through tough times together and creating the culture, norms, and structure of true community. Community is complicated. It's imperfect. But it's real life… engaging, empowering and exhilarating.

I've seen too many times the way that hospitality and amenity-based senior living turns capable citizens into helpless consumers. I've heard residents in expensive and breathtakingly beautiful senior living communities refer to themselves as inmates. They're not locked in their living areas, of course. What they're talking about is how it feels to live in a place where one has no decision-making power. This "doing for" approach worms its way into how people receive care and services in their homes as well. Society, as a whole, has bought into the notion we must take our hands off the wheel when it comes to our care and well-being as we grow older and that we have to trade in autonomy and self-efficacy when we need supportive services.

The Eden Alternative, the non-profit organization I lead, began in the mid-90's with a mission to eliminate the loneliness, helplessness and boredom that exists in institutional nursing homes. Since then, we've expanded our reach and our work —to address any place where elders live— because it's not just nursing home residents that suffer. The hospitality model can institutionalize people…by doing too much "for" and not enough "with." Too often, we limit people by focusing on who they were in the past instead of future growth, and by programming and designing "experiences" instead of creating a culture where meaning springs from those who live in the community.

It's interesting that's the route we've taken in creating living environments for older people. There's no research or data that I'm aware of that supports the notion that we live longer or better when we have "carefree" lives of catered-to "convenience." There is, however, an abundance of research that shows that we age well when we have meaningful and purposeful roles to play, when we challenge ourselves intellectually and when we're deeply connected to other people and something bigger than ourselves.

I'm very encouraged that there's a shift happening in the field of senior living, but there's still work to be done. Cohousing, and in particular Quimper Village, is at the cutting edge.

I spent much of my career as a senior living leader focused on providing great care, services and amenities. My leadership team and I owned the decision-making and "fixed" all of the problems. Quimper Village residents "fix" their own problems more efficiently and much more effectively than any leadership team I've encountered. And in doing so, they benefit from lives of purpose, meaning and connectedness. Read on, see what they did (it's profound) and how they did it.

INTRODUCTION

IN 1992, MDA ARCHITECTS converted an old, dilapidated industrial building in an urban part of Emeryville, California, into a new cohousing community. Doyle Street Cohousing was, and still is, a very successful community. I loved living there for twelve years.

There were waves of queries early on from people who were interested in learning more about the cohousing concept and rehabbing an old building, and the community was inundated with visitors and questions. At first, the residents didn't consider the one-visitor-at-a-time policy to be too much. Then, after about two years, they said, "No more." And it made sense. It was inconvenient and a distraction to the community. This budding new neighborhood grew weary of the attention and wanted to focus on fostering their own community and getting on with their lives.

Doyle Street Cohousing received a lot of attention from folks who wanted to learn how to rehabilitate derelict and abandoned buildings, and to transform them into vibrant, livable environments. The residents of the development were not prepared to give detailed seminars for accomplishing urban rehabilitation projects. We answered incoming questions in curtailed, cryptic, and anecdotal fashion. Consequently, few projects like Doyle Street Cohousing have been created in North America, despite their extraordinary affordability.

We should have written a book then about Doyle Street Cohousing: the advantages, disadvantages, and how it was done. And we also should have put out a book about each unique, successful cohousing scenario thereafter: Davis, California (suburban); Yarrow, in Chilliwack, BC, Canada (eco village); Santa Cruz, California (new urban); Mountain View, California (bought a single family house and built a 19 unit cohousing on it); and so on. We'd have more cohousing in North America if we'd done so.

This book is a unique and important story of how one group, Quimper

Village, in Port Townsend, Washington, accomplished, start to finish, one project in three years (efficient projects are developed in two to three years). Of course, each community is unique. But sometimes it's a good idea to know exactly how one group did it. Other resident groups who are interested in creating cohousing can use the story of Quimper Village to consciously and deliberately deviate from that clear point of departure: What they did, how they did it, what they'd do differently, and whether or not they felt it was worth it.

The Quimper Village residents are the main authors of this book. But just like a cohousing design process, the editors did what they could to give structure to the story and tell the tale of one project, as clearly, accurately, and concisely as possible. Here are some highlights:

- It was completed in a relatively short time—three years from land purchase to move-in. Some cohousing groups have been completed in two years, but very few. Projects with inexperienced architects take much longer.
- It was a relatively smooth process—a little drama, but not much.
- It was done on budget.
- Most importantly, it's a high-functioning cohousing community. People know each other, care about each other, and reach out to support each other. You feel it when you are there—it's palpable.
- The end result is a high-quality community—most everyone feels they are now living up to their potential, collectively and individually, and are looking forward to happy ever aftering here.

This book also had to be written because it is a state-of-the-art community, a model project really, but in a town that's remote. Our hope is that this book will be seen by aspiring communities more than the QV community itself, and that it will be a source of inspiration for them.

As senior activist Bill Thomas likes to point out, "If you could put twenty seniors on a boat and take them out to a deserted island, they will do a better job of providing for themselves than any institution that we have yet created."

Quimper Village proves this hypothesis. This is the story of their voyage—how they prepared, how they launched, the voyage itself, how they landed, and how they settled.

—Chuck Durrett

One More Thing

The development of a place like Quimper Village (QV) is not linear, but books are. In trying to organize the chapters for this book, we had to come up with an ordered sequence. But in reality, many tracks at QV were moving along simultaneously. People were looking for property while they were building their mailing list, while they were setting up legal structures, and so on. In this regard, creating cohousing is more like cooking a complicated meal. It requires considerable (but not impossible) juggling and constantly changing priorities. But it can be done, and QV is great proof of that!

—Alexandria Levitt

1

"Life is for participating, not for spectating."
— *Kathrine Switzer*

Let's Talk

ONE WEEK IN DECEMBER of 2013, a brief announcement appeared in the adult education program of a Unitarian Universalist (UU) church in Washington State.

It read:

> *The Hundhausens have been thinking about where we want to live in the years ahead. Maybe you have too! How long do we want to (can we) stay in our two-story home? We know we don't want to pay a big corporation for an independent living apartment or an assisted living arrangement. What if we lived in a small complex with our own one or two bedroom homes on one level space? What if it were like-minded friends who owned the other living units around us? What if the complex were built as "green" as we could afford to build it? What if the people living there were in charge of all decisions about the management of the property? What if there was a community house on the property where we could spend time together and eat some meals together? If this interests you at any level, please join us to begin the discussion.*

In a few words, Pat Hundhausen summed up the intangible longing so many of us have for more meaning, more connection, and more community in our lives. We may not even know what that looks like, but we sure know what it feels like because we've experienced it in our lives. Maybe it was a fun and lively dorm experience in college. Maybe it was spending time camping with friends. Maybe it was working on a project for your children's school with thoughtful, engaging people.

With that simple notice, Pat struck a chord in her town. Three years later, Quimper Village (QV) was the result. And it all began with a simple invitation. Let's talk. Let's break bread. Let's discuss what we think

Future QV residents at Study Group One.

our future might be like, and along the way, get to know each other a little bit better.

This all started when Pat looked around at her fellow churchgoers and thought how nice it would be if some of them could live more closely as they aged. Her husband, David, was having some mobility issues, and she wasn't as flexible or energetic as she once was. Even though there was already a strong sense of community at her church, the folks in the congregation really didn't know each other that well. The director of the adult education program heard what Pat was thinking about and asked her to do a presentation. That's what prompted her to write the notice on the previous page.

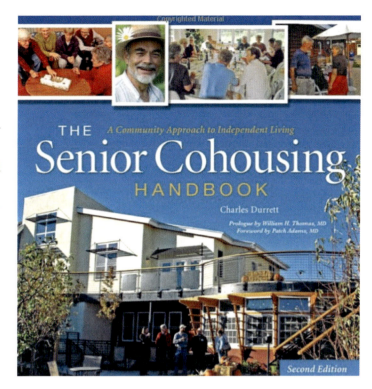

Pat didn't mention the term *cohousing* in her notice because at the time she had never heard of this model, which originated in Denmark. It was a happy coincidence that someone, namely Charles "Chuck" Durrett, had already written a book on cohousing and that he and his partner, Katie McCamant, had pioneered developments all over the country. Pat then found Durrett's book, *The Senior Cohousing Handbook*, before the presentation and she thought what it described sounded pretty interesting—a community where people would share community-owned resources such as a large common house; where they would have meals together frequently and engage in other social activities; where they would live close to one another but have their own home and income; and where they wouldn't become lonely, isolated, or bored as they got older. Pat and David took inspiration from this book, and they got to work to preparing their first presentation.

Sixty-four people showed up to that first presentation at the Quimper Unitarian Universalist Fellowship Church. They wanted to hear Pat talk about this mythical place, Quimper Village. Pat, never a shrinking violet, had taken it upon herself to name the community while it was barely a gleam in her eye.

QV got traction in earnest once most people had read this book.

"We heard a story many, many years ago where some woman was really concerned because they were leaving their town where they lived and moving to another town. And they asked her, 'Well how was it where you lived?' She said, 'Well it was wonderful. We had good friends. We liked the community. We had things to do there.' And the response was, 'Well, that's how you'll feel where you're going.' I love that little story. Were you happy where you were? You'll be happy where you're going. And I think it's what's in you as a person. How are you gonna make it work."

—Ivar Dolph

Right from the start, Pat, a retired teacher of special education and school administrator, and David, a retired associate professor of speech and theater, had an eye for the details and the delivery that encouraged people to connect. They had arranged tables that sat eight apiece, and they angled them to the front. Pat and David began with a small presentation on cohousing, a summary of this option in Denmark, its characteristics, and why it appealed to them personally. They then asked each table of participants to become a small group; to introduce themselves to one another; select a notetaker (each table had been provided a pen and paper); and to answer three questions, going around to each person in the group.

"I might like to live in senior cohousing because . . ."

"I would be worried about living in senior cohousing because . . ."

"Questions I still have about senior cohousing are . . ."

The participants were given forty-five minutes to answer these questions. Then the small groups were asked to return to the big group. The notetaker from each small group reported their responses for each question, not repeating answers from groups who had spoken before. A volunteer recorded the responses on an easel pad in front of the room. They were later typed out and emailed to every participant.

Pat and David then described the next step if people wanted to continue to investigate senior cohousing as an option for their future, which was to enroll in a ten week course titled Study Group 1: Aging Successfully (SG1). Chuck Durrett brought the concept of such a class back from Denmark, and he has found it to be a key tool in developing successful cohousing communities. Pat had prepared a handout for each participant that summarized the ten sessions, and she briefly went over them. There was a sheet on each table that participants could use to sign up to receive an email about when the course would be offered. Pat had not yet set up the

Celebrating all of the small and large successes along the way.

time, date, and location of the SG1 sessions. In retrospect, she thought it would have been helpful if the sessions had already been scheduled.

Pat sent out the emails, and twenty people signed up to take the course. SG1 was to be run through the church's Spring Adult Learning Program. Pat charged $55 each for the workbooks, and she suggested that couples not share workbooks because answers could, and should, be different. Pat purchased the workbooks and facilitator guide ahead of time for the twenty people, and the participants paid her for them later. The church gave them the space to hold the class.

Pat had not taken the SG1 training before she led this workshop. She was coached through it, however, and relied heavily on the manuals; and her experience as a teacher proved to be very helpful. In retrospect, she felt that it would have made more sense for her to have gone through the SG1 facilitator training before leading the workshop. But she didn't want to lose momentum, so she jumped in. Time was of the essence.

For the classes, Pat arranged the tables in a U-shape for the participants. At Durrett's suggestion, she made the room as inviting and pleasant as possible. She brought tablecloths and flowers for the tables every week and a few participants provided light snacks, taking turns. Though the curriculum is well laid out in the workbooks, Pat created her own format. She liked a structured learning environment, so she always began with a check-in. Sometimes Pat did this with a question to get to know each other better, such as, "What is your biggest pet peeve?" Or she would ask an open-ended question about some of the material they were covering, such as, "In a few words, how is where you are living now working for you?" Sometimes she brought in handouts to supplement the course materials.

The most powerful thing in the SG1 class, according to Pat and David, was when they broke up into small groups of three to five people. Pat would prepare two to three thought-provoking questions each week based on the session material, such as "What were the last years of your parents' lives like? What was that like for you?" Each week, people sat with different participants so that by the end of the course, many participants knew each other on a pretty deep level. The last session involved a field trip to an existing cohousing community (more easily done in some parts of the country than others).

Pat could not emphasize enough the importance the SG1 course had in laying the foundation for moving forward to begin building Quimper Village. It was not until the course was over that Pat realized how much people had bonded and shared with one another, and how much alike "we really all were as we face the years ahead."

"I just love the people here. I mean there's just no question about it. There's just a whole variety of people. People in this group have traveled all over. We have four or five engineers in this community, lots of people who are writers and artists, and it's just a rich background. I think of what this means to people that are single here, that I'm close to . . . and for them it's so rich. For instance, if they need something or if they don't want to go by themselves to Seattle—there's always people here that are willing to go. It really adds so much richness as well as support to their lives, all our lives."
—*Kay Darlington*

What was being built here was fundamentally a community of people who could envision embarking on this sort of adventure with each other. When the participants finished the course, everyone wanted to move forward and build a senior cohousing community. Everyone stayed with the project through the summer until the Getting-It-Built Workshop. Some people then dropped out be-

Getting to Know Each Other

Why not try this exercise when first bringing people together? Break up into groups of five or six. Each person takes a turn answering a question posed by the facilitator. The other group members do not speak or cross talk, they simply listen attentively to the person who is speaking.

- What are your greatest aspirations for the last third part of your life?

- What are the greatest fears for the last third part of your life?

What a great way to break the ice and get the conversation going. This exercise also reminds people this is an interactive process in which there are no observers, just participants.

cause their spouses weren't on board, or they determined it would be too expensive for them. Durrett says that typically about 40 percent of the workshop participants go on to build a senior cohousing community. This was true for QV.

> "What I enjoy most about living here is being with the people. It's easy to see somebody. You don't have to put yourself out to do it. You know, Jack and I don't go very often to the Friday Forum, but we did this past time and questions came up that talked about introverts and extroverts, with everybody sitting there and identifying themselves. As an introvert . . . it's easy here to be around people, and you don't have to step out for it to happen. It just is. You're gonna see them for dinner, you're going to see somebody walking down to the car, et cetera. If I get antsy in the house, I'll just come up to the common house to see if anybody's around."
> —Carolyn Salmon

It should be noted that the group held a total of three public presentations about cohousing. The first, previously outlined, presented the basic concept. The second was a panel discussion designed to increase membership in advance of the Getting-It-Built Workshop (see chapter 2). The third involved reaching out to all Unitarian Universalist congregations within a 100-mile radius of Port Townsend (see chapter 2). At the time the group was meeting weekly to have coffee and talk. As new members joined (paying a small fee to show good faith), Pat and David recognized that there was a need to hold a second SG1 workshop. And they did. There was growing enthusiasm for the project, and the group was solidifying. These factors led them to schedule the Getting-It-Built Workshop, a big step forward for the group, and the first sign they were getting really serious.

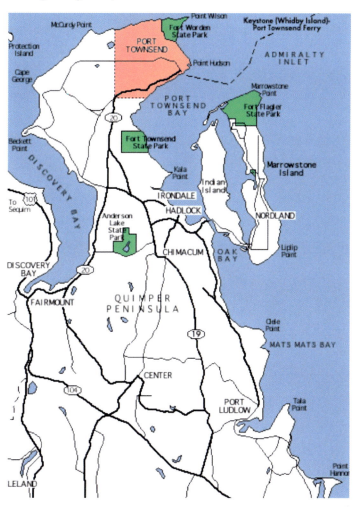

A map of Quimper Peninsula showing the geographic location of Port Townsend.

What Got Them Started

- A public invitation to hear about cohousing at a well-attended Unitarian Church

- A well-attended public presentation (64 people), plus two more presentations

- Two Study Group 1 workshops (10 weeks each) at the same church

A seaport town, Port Townsend has always attracted dreamers, and it's full of people who act on those dreams.

Why Quimper Village?

Selecting the name of a cohousing group can be a tricky process. It shouldn't sound too alternative or too much like a commune. Leaving out the word "cohousing" is not a bad idea, either. In fact, doing so can help you overcome some bureaucratic hurdles. For example, a bank will ask you about your name every time you need a loan. The term "cohousing" invariably opens the door to questions. Continually explaining the cohousing concept can unnecessarily slow the process and sometimes lead to objections. At the same time, you want something that captures a bit of the spirit of this particular adventure.

In the case of QV, Pat selected the word Quimper because it is the name of the peninsula where the community was to be located in the town of Port Townsend. It looks a bit like the top of a seahorse and is named after the Peruvian-born Spanish explorer, Manuel Quimper, who charted the north and south coasts of the Strait of Juan de Fuca during the summer of 1790.

Deciding the name yourself is not an example of dynamic governance at work! But Pat was sort of the Mama Bear of this cohousing vision, and in the end people couldn't come up with something better. So the name stuck.

Faces of a few residents interviewed for the book.

2

"Whatever good things we build end up building us."
— *Jim Rohn*

The Getting-It-Built Workshop

RIDING HIGH ON THE SUCCESS of the Study Group 1: Aging Successfully classes, the Quimper Village folks decided to take a big leap into the future and arrange a Getting-It-Built Workshop.

The aim of the QV group was to hold the workshop at the end of September 2014. This meant they had to raise the money for the workshop, a not insignificant sum of $6,000. In the meantime, they needed to come up with $1,000 to pay McCamant & Durrett Architects in order to retain the September dates they wanted. One of the QV members offered to put up the retainer, and their contribution was reflected later as costs were amortized among the participants.

QV mailed the check immediately, and by doing so, committed themselves to recruiting enough participants to pay the total $6,000 workshop fee. They also needed to add members to their fledgling community, and for that they needed a marketing plan. They now had a deadline, a membership quota, and a fundraising goal they were committed to meet.

They began to use their regular meetings for marketing tasks and membership development. These activities were, in effect, community-building opportunities. The term "build community" is used over and over when discussing the development of a cohousing neighborhood. This term refers not just to the physical setting or to accumulating a lot of names for a mailing list, but to the "human community." Building community refers to the bonds that hold the group together, the friendships that enable neighbor to help neighbor, and not just giving help but accepting it when needed as well. As more than one resident said, "If you can't build this kind of community, why bother to develop the property?"

One of the members volunteered to set up a website so they could

Katie McCamant, with Chuck Durrett, at the all important Getting-It-Built Workshop. This is where QV first learned how to work as a group, what the process looks like, how to get their money in and out, and if they hadn't already, how to find land.

market the Getting-It-Built Workshop and introduce their planned village to others searching for cohousing on the internet. An application form for the workshop was posted there. They also advertised a public presentation that would take place at their Unitarian Universalist Fellowship church, this one in the evening. Besides telling their story and presenting information about cohousing, the presentation involved a panel discussion that featured members of their group. This discussion was followed by a Q & A session. QV members made sure to ask folks who attended this presentation to register and provide their contact information. The QV contact database was increasing.

Since the group was being sponsored by their UU Fellowship, they decided to invite UU members from the surrounding area to come to Port Townsend for a weekend. The activities included a city tour, a theater event, a potluck supper, and, of course, a cohousing presentation (presentation number three!). They sent an email and a flyer to all the UU Fellowship churches within a hundred-mile radius of Port Townsend. Though only nine people responded to the invitation, one couple wound up becoming members of the cohousing community.

Besides the website and the public presentations, QV distributed flyers that advertised the workshop at

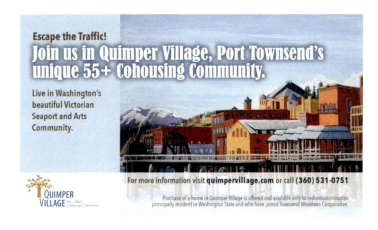

their local farmers market. They also posted flyers on bulletin boards around town. As a result, thirty-five people signed up for the workshop. This turnout provided enough funds to cover the cost of the workshop, and there was still enough money left over to provide lunch on one of the two days, as well as snacks on both days.

While QV was busy recruiting participants for the Getting-It-Built Workshop (at this point, new members were only asked to contribute a one-time fee of $50

An example of QV's business/marketing cards.

Example of QV's advertising efforts at a local movie theater.

The site that became QV, located along a popular footpath, called out to the founding members.

to cover basic operating costs), one of their members was researching properties in Port Townsend which, though not for sale, were sufficiently large to accommodate a cohousing community. She contacted nine owners, and was surprised to discover that most of them were interested in selling their land.

Prior to the Getting-It-Built Workshop, QV established initial criteria for a desirable site. The group identified eight possible sites from the list provided by the member who researched the properties, and narrowed the list down to two. Therefore, during the workshop weekend, the group could actually walk around the two properties with Durrett and McCamant, who would then give QV their opinion about the feasibility of building on each. There will be more on site selection in chapter eight.

To take full advantage of having Durrett and McCamant in Port Townsend, QV scheduled another public presentation (number four!) to be held the night before the workshop. Once again, they asked folks to register when they came in. This added more people to their growing contact list. McCamant and Durrett's presentation was well attended and they did a good job of combining slides and narration to tell the cohousing story. To capitalize even more on their visit, QV arranged for Durrett to be interviewed on the local radio station. These events helped generate interest in the project within the vicinity.

QV's confidence to move ahead

was inspired by the bonds they built during their SG1 sessions. That, in turn, helped them prepare for the Getting-It-Built Workshop. The Getting-It-Built Workshop, in turn, helped focus their energy so that they could create the organizational structure and project timelines needed to actually build their cohousing community. This workshop gave QV the roadmap for their cohousing journey. With it, they could make their dream a reality.

In addition to discussing the design and construction processes, the Getting-It-Built Workshop covers four important concepts for creating cohousing. It teaches resident groups to:

1. Follow the critical path. Development is a process and groups need to keep their focus on the critical path: do this, then this, then do this. Don't get distracted.
2. Hire the professionals they need. This will save time and money.
3. Establish clear organizational structure and governance processes, including decision making.
4. Clarify membership criteria and processes.

At the end of the second day of the workshop, Durrett made a list of committees (QV uses the term teams) they would need to get started. Folks were invited to sign up. These teams included:

- Site (searches for the property for the community)
- Finance and Legal
- Process (how the group makes decisions)
- Marketing/PR/Membership
- Coordinating (made up of the leaders of the other teams and leads the whole effort; they make sure that all work is coordinated and everything is getting done).

QV spreading the message at the annual parade in Port Townsend.

QV subsequently added other teams: Neighborhood Relations, Social, E-Communications, Design, Landscape, and Community Agreements. All members served on at least one team.

QV set the tone for how they functioned as a group long before scheduling the Getting-It-Built Workshop. It's important to remember that they decided to go through with the workshop before they had all the people and funds they needed. They pushed while they planned and strived to work one, two, or three steps ahead of where they were in terms of membership and money. They just assumed they would be able to do it, and they did. The risk was that if they didn't succeed, the folks who were in as founding members would have to bear the cost.

"To take the step of having a Getting-It-Built Workshop really launches the project and keeps things moving. If you have it, it's highly motivating."
— David Hundhausen

After the workshop, QV continued to meet weekly. To further educate themselves, they invited a wide range of guests that included a general contractor, an architect, a commercial loan officer, a real estate attorney, a member of another cohousing community, and other professionals. These guests explained their roles in development and construction, and detailed what the group needed to consider on each topic. Group members asked numerous questions about costs, processes, governmental regulations, and so forth.

As mentioned earlier, after the SG1 classes, everyone who remained in the group wanted to move forward and build a senior cohousing community. Nine of the twenty participants of SG1 also participated in the Getting-It-Built Workshop (the others having dropped out for various reasons). These nine people represented five households; the twelve who had left represented twelve households.

The Getting-It-Built Workshop taught residents how to make decisions efficiently and effectively as a group.

This Is How McCamant & Durrett Architects and CoHousing Solutions Advertises a Getting-It-Built Workshop

The **Getting-It-Built Workshop (GIB)** provides a clear overview of the cohousing development process, covering development strategies, timelines, financing options, raising money, working together, and outreach and recruitment to give the group the tools to effectively plan their next steps. In addition to customizing the workshop to fit specific needs, the GIB also covers:

The Cohousing Process
- An overview of the development process, from initial meetings to moving in.
- Forming and organizing a group, working together, and issues to address early in the process.
- Development scenarios—the group's role, consultant's roles, and options for finding and working with a developer.

The Technical Issues
- Money—getting money in and getting money out of the project.
- Financing options, ownership structures, and financial realities. (What will it cost?)
- Designing for community—design issues.

Working Together
- How does the group organize to make decisions effectively?
- Getting along—the dynamics of group interaction and reaching potential.
- How to become a lean, clean cohousing machine.

What Next?
- Am I ready? What do we do now? Next steps.
- The individual's role, the group's role, and the role of professionals.
- Which committees/teams do I join?

Workshop Fee:
$6,000 (standard/general) or $10,000 (site specific) in U.S. dollars, plus travel expenses for two people (we are glad to stay in people's homes to keep expenses down). We provide some assistance to help you organize and promote the workshop, including a prep checklist, a sample press release and flyer, promotion through our media channels, and of course all workshop materials for attendees. We're also happy to do a public presentation at no extra cost on the Friday night prior to the workshop.

3

"Coming together is a BEGINNING. Staying together is PROGRESS. And, working together is SUCCESS."
— Henry Ford

Be Part of the Team

WHEN QUIMPER VILLAGE started getting the word out about their planned neighborhood, they quickly realized they had a big hill to climb. For many in the general public, cohousing was a totally unfamiliar concept. For some, it sounded like a hippie commune. That notion could unfairly send them running away from QV.

Designing Our Image

QV had to counteract these misconceptions and negative associations as they spread the word about their new neighborhood. To do so, they got their name out early and in as many ways as they could think of. Soon, lots of folks started to say, "Oh, Quimper Village, I've heard of that. It's some kind of new housing development." This was evidence they were going in the right direction, but what kind of housing development? To lessen confusion and increase their appeal, QV came up with some slogans with emotional heft. For example:

- "What could be more audacious than twenty-eight households deciding to build their own neighborhood?"
- "Quimper Village, Be part of the Dream!"
- "Downsize and simplify your lives."

They put these phrases on their website as soon as they were able to get it up and running.

A logo was also critical. Logos can originate from clip art, but having a graphic artist create one is a better idea. This is what QV did. The artist created several to choose from, and they were presented to the members. Their favorite depicted a tree beside the name Quimper Village. Once adopted, this logo appeared on their website and all of their marketing materials.

Not surprisingly, an online presence was essential to their marketing efforts. A website with photos of an active project demonstrates the difference between a project that is only a dream and one that is a real enterprise with real people, real land, and real architectural drawings.

While QV was in the marketing stage, their website dealt with things people needed to know if they wanted to become part of the village before it was built. Topics included: What you need to do to become a member?

- Attend some meetings
- Observe a team
- Come to a social event

How do members financially contribute to the development of the community?

Quimper Village changed its website once the project was complete and the residents moved into their new homes.

Today their website (www.quimpervillage.com) features:

- A page that describes Port Townsend, with links to some of its attractions
- A page that contains photos and brief biographies of all the members
- A page that contains links to other cohousing communities and relevant resources
- A page where readers can sign up to receive the community newsletter (all their newsletters are also archived on their website)
- A page featuring QV homes when they come up for sale

- By making contributions that would eventually be equal to their down payment.

Marketing Tools That Worked

There are many different marketing tools, and choosing which to use depends on the target market. For example, Port Townsend is a community of 9,000 people, most of them older, who relocated for their retirement. Marketing to a captive group of retired folks living in a small town is certainly different than marketing to the same age group in a large urban area. There is a lot less "noise" to compete with.

As mentioned earlier, QV did four presentations in Port Townsend when they were recruiting new members and generating interest in the Getting-It-Built Workshop. All of these were held at the same UU Fellowship church. Their "dog and pony show" about the hopes and expectations of their neighborhood provided an immediacy, chemistry, and legitimacy that no online presence could mimic.

A big change to marketing via public presentations occurred after QV acquired their site and after the conceptual designs for their village were created, which they then mounted on large display boards. Having a site to show people, whether in the form of a drawing or by actually visiting the site, is a great marketing tool on its own. It makes the possibility of a home start to become real. QV took the conceptual drawings with them whenever they did a public presentation. They also produced a color brochure that included a site plan and floor plans of the three different-sized homes. These were handed out to those who attended their presentations.

What proved effective for QV were public presentations in neighboring communities. It's hard to overemphasize their importance for the development of QV. It proved to be one of their most basic and important marketing tools. With these new marketing materials, they held public presentations across

The homepage for QV's website. The residents helped design the logo and page layout.

the water in the Seattle suburb of Edmonds at a UU Fellowship church, and in the unincorporated community of Chimacum. They did the same in the nearby towns of Sequim and Port Angeles too. They chose these locations because they were geographically close. The presentation in Chimacum was held at a community center, the one in Sequim was held in the home of one of the QV members, and the one in Port Angeles was at their city library. They never had to pay for the use of any of these facilities, and they publicized them through flyers placed on bulletin boards, announcements posted in the community calendars of newspapers, online calendars of radio stations, and on the group's website.

"There is a yin and yang. You want households to be committed. You want to sell all of these houses, and yet some people shouldn't be part of this type of village. Either their personality or what they are looking for isn't going to fit and blend. One gal wanted to move in, and she thought it was more of an assisted living, where you each help each other with that. And I said to her, 'No, we're looking for what you would be contributing to the community.'"
— Janet Palmer

The QV folks tried a lot of other ways to garner name recognition too. They managed to get their reluctant local newspaper to publish a few stories about the group, and they encouraged a local magazine, *3rd Act*, to publish a personal story of how one of their members found his way to QV. They purchased ads in a summer tourism magazine published by their newspaper and in theatre and concert programs for local groups that attracted audience members from outside Port Townsend. They even sponsored the local radio station for three months. They made magnetic signs for their cars, and different members swapped them so they'd cover more ground. They created bumper stickers too, but they only used a few of them because they had neglected to include a disclaimer required by the state of Washington.

Members wore buttons inviting people to ask about QV. They participated in a parade with several members carrying a banner bearing "Quimper Village," while their tallest member, wearing a stovepipe hat, rode on the back of a convertible and waved at the crowd. This appearance was so noticeable that it netted them a new member household. They had

The QV group at a seminar learning how to take care of their property after move-in.

A QV advertisement that ran in local movie theaters. Created by Isabel Bay Designs.

booths at a local home and garden show and at the Jefferson County Fair.

They even contracted with a popular local movie theater to participate in their on-screen, preshow advertising program. QV provided the theater with up to three different slides, which were put into a rotation of advertisements shown before the movies. This was not an expensive program, and QV did two, one-month periods of on-screen ads. Some people who had seen these slides at the theater did, in fact, come to their meetings.

Some of these marketing tools provided not only name recognition, but also public education about their project. They answered common questions about Quimper Village, cohousing, and related topics from a wide range of people who had seen their advertisements.

"I think that when people go into that empty nester stage, looking forward to the kids getting out and on their own, they don't think of cohousing. They think about, 'Well, we'll travel the world.' So it's the long-term thing that needs to be addressed. One man, around 70, came by at a booth that we had set up at a fair and he showed some interest. So we offered him our brochure and he said, 'Oh no. I'll think about this later. I'm too young.' So it is kind of an attitude, and we had to convince him, 'Hey, this is not assisted living. This is a participatory community where you have to be part of developing it, building it, and maintaining it.'

—*Mack Boelling*

QV's monthly newsletter was, and remains, its major source of advertising for the community. It's done by a team using a simple free online service. Their newsletter attracted a lot of interest in the project, interest that resulted in folks asking to be added to their mailing list and/or requesting more information than was contained on the QV website. The name and contact information of each person who inquired was added to their database. Creating and distributing the newsletter before a site was even selected was essential, and it made the project feel more real.

The other really successful marketing tool was QV's monthly Coffee and Conversation sessions. They were conducted Saturday mornings from 10 a.m. until noon, by reservation, and were held in Pat and David Hundhausen's home. These were advertised on the QV website and in the community calendars of the local newspapers. The couple provided their phone number, because they wanted to know how many people they could expect. They always served fresh bakery items with coffee and tea, and they prepared name tags for everyone in attendance.

They began each session by having folks introduce themselves and tell the group what they knew about cohousing in general and about the QV project in particular. Pat and David would tell their personal story, and then about QV and how it was being developed. They showed the guests conceptual drawings and also the books that had been produced following each of the development workshops. They gave everyone a color brochure that described QV. This brochure also included floor plans of the three different sizes of homes they planned to build.

They wanted to show visitors how much serious work had been done and give them confidence that this was a project worth joining. Of course the visitors were given the opportunity to ask questions and raise concerns. Almost everyone who attended one of these sessions attended a general community meeting. Critically, most of the folks who became members of the QV community had attended a Coffee and Conversation session in the Hundhausen home. David considered it to be their most successful marketing tool.

Chuck leading a group during the design workshop.

Most cohousing groups do something similar, but for the most part, they meet in local restaurants. For the QV folks, these sessions in a private home provided a different atmosphere. A home is warm and inviting, free of the noise and activity of a crowded business. And most importantly, it shows how much skin in the game Pat and David had—inviting strangers into their home to discuss the project in a personal way.

Marketing Tools That Didn't Work

QV did consider reaching out to the greater Seattle area for members, especially because they knew that folks of retirement age might be interested in QV for several reasons. Most notably, Port Townsend was already a popular weekend getaway destination (it's only a short ferry ride away from Seattle) and the cost of housing in Port Townsend is considerably less than it is across the Sound.

QV placed ads in *Prime Time*, a Seattle magazine, and conducted a short Google AdWords campaign. Google AdWords is a service that simplifies online advertising and helps people find what they're searching for. Folks who type in any of the words you provide to Google are given a display that contains your website address and a brief description of what it contains. If people click through to your site, you pay for the click. To control costs, you can set a dollar limit on what you're willing to spend over a specified period of time. QV saw increased traffic to their website as a result of the program, but they did

Online Marketing

For any new cohousing project, an online presence is important. It helps people learn about a project in development and it gives a growing community a terrific platform to explain their mission, show off their real estate, put in a plug for new members, and advertise. This can be simultaneously done on the community's own website, plus on social media like Facebook, Twitter, and Instagram—whatever works best and where new members are likely to be.

It is important that someone in the core group has the skills to produce a website. If not, it will be worth the money to pay someone to do it, provided they work with the community's input. Regardless, updates should be easy to create and manage, because the website must constantly evolve as the project evolves. Facebook is certainly user-friendly, and putting up a page there for the community is straightforward enough.

In the case of the community website and Facebook page, having ***lots of photos*** is important. Add some video too, if there is a wonderful event going on. It's never been easier to catch a snippet of something. You never know, that moment may be what convinces someone to join the neighborhood.

not gain any further inquiries or members from Seattle. Even though it increased traffic, they abandoned it after a month.

Ultimately, marketing was not hard for the members of QV. They simply put their unique and hard-won skills from their previous careers to work on the project. They never needed a hard sell. They just had to be themselves and let their enthusiasm for the project show. As David Hundhausen said, "Just pick up the phone, 'Hey, how ya doing? Do you need to know more?' It was really about using the phone." In fact, for a long time, David's personal phone number was on the website, and he still gets calls for QV.

Why Marketing AND Sales Matter

When potential cohousing residents are asked to choose committees— or in this case, teams— to work on, there is never a shortage for people who want to serve on the Design Committee. Staffing up the Marketing Committee, on the other hand, is always a challenge. Marketing is one of the most important and critical pieces of this work. If enthusiasm lags, the group can expect a nosedive in terms of sales. People may feel uncomfortable with marketing. Also, they may be unfamiliar with how sales duties really work, and why a good marketing approach is so important.

It's easy to think that the idea of your cohousing community will be so appealing to everyone that you won't have any trouble recruiting thirty households. But the reality is quite different, because cohousing is still relatively unfamiliar to most Americans. This is why old-fashioned marketing and sales work is crucial.

How QV Rocked Their Marketing Efforts

- Scheduled a regular, bimonthly, all-member meeting that was always open to visitors (Process Team).
- Set up a webpage and Facebook page that were continually updated.
- Marketed the slogan, "Quimper Village, Be Part of the Dream" at different times with flyers at their local farmers market and around town, newspaper articles, opinion pieces, ads, local radio interviews, and even a QV car in a local parade. They also made business cards, brochures, bumper stickers, logo pins, and relied on word of mouth (Marketing Team).
- Held monthly Coffee and Conversation sessions in a private home for people who were interested in joining. These sessions were used to describe the latest updates to the QV project and answer questions (Marketing Team).
- Created a monthly newsletter that provided fun and interesting news about the project while it was under development. After QV was complete, the newsletter changed to provide information on how life is progressing at there. It also serves as their way to advertise houses that come up for sale.
- Provided a phone number on the website, which people could call to learn more about Quimper Village.

An Interview with David Hundhausen
By Chuck Durrett and Alexandria Levitt

Chuck: During these Coffee and Conversation sessions, you basically hand-hold people through consciousness-raising and out of denial. How do you do that in two hours?

What you have to do is let people talk about their expectations. They envision their own future and what's typical in our culture—this is what happens when you get older and this is what you do. But it's really a completely different thing to do, to make the decision, to go into a senior cohousing community where you're going to have the kinds of support that are really not provided in any of the other kinds of environments.

Chuck: So here you are sitting with prospective members for two hours of coffee and conversation. What questions would you ask them to get them to talk?

Well, one of the things we would ask would be, "How did you hear about cohousing? What do you know about it? How do you feel about it?" Then we would explain how we heard about it, you know, share our story. But really you need to find out where they are before you talk about where you want to go with them.

Alexandria: How did they hear about your coffee conversations?

We did it every Saturday morning. We placed a notice in the newspaper with my home phone number so people could call up, and they did. We would know who was coming. Sometimes people asked questions on the phone and we could answer some of them. But sometimes we would just say, "Please come to our meeting and we will deal with some of these concerns that you have. We'll have coffee and some bakery goods. It'll be a nice morning."

Chuck: How many people moved in here that started with the coffee?

Practically everybody after the two Study Group 1 sessions, which brought in about sixteen families. Most everybody else had been at a Coffee and Conversation. We invited people to come to our general meetings, and they would show up and they would check in.

4

"There is no power for change greater than a community discovering what it cares about."
— *Margaret J. Wheatley*

Building a Community

SOMETHING THE RESIDENTS of Quimper Village learned right away was that they were not just building houses, they were building a community. Every time there was an opportunity to bring folks together, they did it in a thoughtful and appealing way.

Because the residents of QV had made these activities enjoyable, they had also created "community glue" (so named by intentional community expert, Diana Leafe Christian). They had fun together—wine and cheese after a meeting, game days, picnics, and holiday parties.

"Bill and I were looking for exactly this lifestyle, and we'd been looking for a couple of years. We didn't think it was possible, and we didn't want to move because my whole family, including my kids and grandkids are here.

And we said, 'It's not going to happen.' We knew that there was cohousing in Bainbridge and up in Bellingham, but we're not moving. And then this [Quimper Village] happened. Before we fully made our commitment, we put the $500 down, which made us an associate member. We went to some meetings and some group activities, enough to find out if this was the kind of group we wanted to live with. It isn't intergenerational (which we wanted because we're real involved with our grandkids). As it turned out, this summer there were tons of kids around and that allayed my fears. . . . Well, we were in denial too about our age and we thought we're really not old enough to be a part of some old retirement group, but that's not what it's like here."

— Kay Darlington

Traditional Development vs. Cohousing Development

When a traditional developer creates a multifamily project, they do many of the things that members of a cohousing community do: secure property, hire the appropriate professionals, get permits, secure construction financing, hire a general contractor, and so on. They even market the houses. What they would not do is:
- Involve the future owners in designing the project
- Build the "people" and create a sense of community
- Establish a governance structure and decision-making process

These are the attributes of a cohousing group, and they are central to what makes this kind of community different from traditional projects. Diana Leafe Christian, one of several consultants on intentional community governance, says there are three management components necessary for a well-functioning community:
- Effective project management
- Community glue— a feeling of connection to others, generated by shared joyous experiences
- Strong process and communication skills, including nonviolent communications and restorative circles

People don't generally love meetings, but the QV Membership Team saw them, especially in the beginning, as a valuable recruiting and marketing tool. At the outset they met once a week, and because everyone wore name tags, it didn't take long to learn names. That weekly contact with persons who could be neighbors produced bonds of trust. And that trust was essential later when big decisions had to be made. QV made their meetings open to visitors, who were then introduced by the Membership Team. Immediately, these visitors sensed a welcoming atmosphere. They joined the meeting circle and had an opportunity to experience the group's professionalism.

An Interview with Mack Boelling
By Chuck Durrett & Alexandria Levitt

Mack: We wanted the visitors to have a good experience so we took a personal approach. We'd always ask the visitors, "Why don't you come fifteen minutes early so we can meet you?" And then I'd ask the members that, if you're able to, come before the meeting begins and talk to new visitors. And visitors didn't participate in the meeting until they became associates, but we would always go around at the end of the meeting before closing and ask them to say something. We wanted to show them how we do business and how we conduct our meetings, and if that was something they found attractive, or if they didn't like it, then that was okay too.

Chuck: They sort of self-qualified.

Mack: Certainly, if you get uncomfortable with direct communication with people that you know, then it might not be for you. You said this many times that this was a self-selecting process, and we presented it that way. Here's who we are. This is what we do. And if you're interested, that's great; we'll talk to you more. We never rejected anybody. But we left it open for them to feel that. They might express, "You know I had a nice meeting, but I'm really not interested. This is not my thing."

Chuck: You don't have to reject people because they'll figure it out for themselves.

Mack: Right. And not only that, the other thing that we always stress is that we don't do any hard sells. You don't want to sell something and then have to live with them the rest of your life if it isn't their thing. And then if someone was really showing interest, we might make a little bit of an outreach and encourage him or her to come back for another visit. Or just occasionally give them a call to check in and see if they have any questions.

The Importance of Using Your Skill Set to Create Your Committees

QV educated themselves extensively about cohousing, and then created the committees (they called them teams) that provided a foundation for all their subsequent efforts. They were fortunate to have members that included two former business owners (one had been a mayor), an engineer, a number of educators, a writer and local historian, a manager (not sales) with a national insurance company, a research microbiologist, an MBA, a personal financial planner, and an environmental regulator. Note: Dig deep into the members' backgrounds—there are sure to be people with knowledge and skills that will be important for a growing community.

Chuck showing the group how to conduct an efficient meeting.

QV ran their meetings in the tradition of dynamic governance (more on that in chapter 6). This meant that their meetings began with a simple "check-in" process and, at the end of the meeting, a "check-out" process. This could be as simple as saying, "I'm delighted to be here," or, "I had to take my dog to the vet this morning." Though the visitors weren't members, their voices were heard, and by witnessing the way QV ran their meetings, potential new members gained confidence that the team was working toward their goal efficiently and effectively.

> *"At the very beginning I went to that initial panel meeting and it was kind of, "Oh yeah, this is what I want. These are the people I want to be with. I want them near me. I want to feel safe and secure. I can contribute to this community. I work with them in the church. This is a perfect fit for me. There is no weighing of benefits or risks. I was ready to jump on board. It hit, timing-wise, perfectly. It couldn't get built fast enough."*
>
> —Janet Palmer

Some members lived out of town. This naturally presented challenges. Knowing that there is nothing like face-to-face, in-person contact, especially when talking about living side by side someday, QV discovered that the best thing was to invite the members from beyond Port

Townsend to stay in the local QV member's homes when they visited. This helped them get to know each other, connect with each other, and reinforce that community glue that helped them build their village.

> "*I think I told you that when we were working on the shop [the woodshop at QV] I would just drive down and walk on the ferry and somebody [from QV] picked me up, and then we'd come and work on the shop and I'd be back on the ferry at three o'clock and back home at Anacortes at five. I did that two or three times a month for six months.*"
>
> "*We had about seven men who were working on and off building the shop and the walls and the storage area. So that's a good way to get to know each other. Before then we would come twice a month on the ferry to a general meeting. And then when the forum started we would stay overnight for the forum. So we asked people if we could stay with them. Mostly people said, "Sure, come and stay with us," so we stayed in maybe six homes and got to know people that way. So by the time we moved here we knew everybody in twenty-eight homes.*"
>
> —Ivar Dolph

Since everyone was expected to participate on at least one team, the out-of-towners were naturally limited in their ability to attend team meetings (though many went to great lengths and did a lot of driving to do so). For those who couldn't make it, QV used speaker phones to include folks who couldn't be there in person. Though they were far away, they could still participate in the meetings, which made them feel connected to their fellow villagers. QV also sent everyone minutes of both the general meetings and the team meetings. Even the minutes created community glue.

The structures are just the picture frame. The people at the heart of them are what really matter.

While meetings themselves were critical to get QV built, the socializing opportunities they created were vitally important too. QV held small group dinners that consisted of six or eight people who would get together at one member's home. The host provided the entrée and the others brought salad, a side dish, or dessert. Since it was difficult for some people to get together at night, they also had small group lunches or brunches, often followed by games. Sometimes there were spontaneous movie nights, or they might make plans to attend cultural events like plays or concerts.

Once QV secured their site, their activities took on a whole new dimension. The site, located in a meadow outside of downtown Port Townsend, was a idyllic. The QV meadow provided a great location for picnics, though the biggest and most exciting event was their groundbreaking ceremony in July, 2016.

Invited to this celebration were the members of the larger community who had played a role in getting QV to the point where they were ready to start construction. These guests included the deputy mayor, the head of Port Townsend's planning commission, the project manager, various civic representatives, the owner of the construction company they planned to use, representatives of their lender, and members of their local chamber of commerce. QV was on its way.

An Interview with Chuck Durrett & Janet Palmer

Chuck: It also pays to have a few people who are impatient, just like it pays to have a few people who don't have too much money because it forces you to stay on budget. The impatient people strive to make the process deliberate, because that goes faster.

Janet: Well it was Pat nagging. "Where's the critical path. Get back to the critical path. It's not on the critical path. Forget the churn. Stay on the critical path."

The minute I walked into the general meeting, you know, that was it. I just fell in love. Then it was about the competency of the people. I could see that these people were getting things done. It was really important that I saw how the meetings were run and how decisions were made and the fun and laughter that was walking into it was great.

—*Araya Sol*

The Importance of the Critical Path

Any project of consequence has to have a clear order of operation. Participants must understand what needs to be addressed and in what order to keep the project progressing on schedule. Establishing a critical path also helps participants avoid the pitfalls of distraction. Durrett spent about twenty-four nights at Pat and David's house during the development of QV. After dinner each night, she'd sit him down in the most comfortable chair and say, "Now, let's go through the critical path. Are we doing what we should be doing? And what's the next step?" This laser-like focus on the critical path was fundamental to this project coming in on time and on budget. This is not necessarily typical, but Chuck was happy to do it because Pat was so motivated to keep moving forward, and she understood the importance of avoiding distractions. For example, she knew that it wasn't the time to talk about kitchen counters or paint colors, not when they still had to get the project approved so they could start interviewing contractors. That opportunity would come later, in eight weeks, so it wasn't worth being distracted by those issues.

The point is that every step matters along the way. The job is not to manage the emergencies, but to manage to avoid the emergencies.

The ground breaking was a time for celebration. No matter how short the design process is, it's too long - because more than anything else the design process builds anticipation and excitement about the next step — building it!

5

"If you want to go fast, go alone; if you want to go far go together."
— *African Proverb*

Professional Partnerships

THE DEVELOPMENT SIDE of Quimper Village was on a fast track from the beginning. Their motto was, "We don't buy green bananas, let's make things happen." Their goal was to move in within three years of the decision to build Quimper Village. In order to do so, they had to quickly address the legal and financial requirements for building the physical neighborhood.

Based on what they learned from their local experts, and at the Getting-It-Built Workshop, and through assessing their own backgrounds, they decided they could be their own developer. This would save them a considerable amount of money and enable them to have more control of the processes and outcomes. They determined that, like many seniors, they had some specific resources that younger folks don't have. Access to these resources made it easier for them to develop their senior cohousing community. These resources included:

- Most of them had figured out what really mattered in their lives. They were quick to assess what compromises they needed to make, even if it meant accepting something they might not prefer or giving up something they favored. Their ability to compromise meant that, as a group, they could reach decisions in a timely manner. This, in turn, meant they avoided long and fruitless discussions about every single detail.
- Most of the members were retired and had time to devote to a project of this size.
- They had all kinds of life experiences and skills that were useful when developing their cohousing project. These included financial services, business ownership, researching and writing, IT skills, counseling, teaching, project managing, and more.
- They had stable incomes from predictable sources: pensions, Social Security, IRAs, and other reliable sources. This meant they would be able to purchase the homes when they were completed.
- They had accumulated financial assets they could draw on, such as equity in their current homes, retirement savings, and other investments for the down payment and financing of the project.
- They had good credit and could qualify for mortgages, and to help guarantee a construction

When Not to Be Your Own Developer

Many cohousing groups partner with a professional developer who, in addition to providing expertise, may have access to land, a strong financial statement, and can guarantee a construction loan. Don't be your own developer if you don't have professionals who have been through the process dozens of times. Don't be your own developer if you can't stomach risk. You might save money if you are your own developer and have consultants who, like Katie and Chuck, know exactly what they are doing.

loan, if necessary.

It was a big responsibility to decide to be one's own developer, but that is what worked for QV. They were not attorneys, professional builders or bankers. They had some glitches along the way, but they were able to correct those with little loss of time and extra cost. They took advice where it was needed and were grateful to all of the professionals who worked with and for them, especially for their willingness to work with amateurs.

Building QV's Professional Partnerships

It became obvious to the group early on that they would need a local project manager with extensive experience in development, construction, and permitting in the local area. In cohousing, the project manager must also be able to work with a team of lay folks on a continuing basis. This was particularly important in the case of QV, because the resident group was working as their own developer. The group hired an experienced contractor to be their project manager. This contractor was familiar with the way the city's building department functioned and also knew some of the subcontractors who had been hired to work on the project. His first task was to help the residents evaluate the different pieces of property they had identified for buildability and permitting concerns.

The group also retained a:
- Local real estate development

Signing the construction contract with Fairbank Construction.

- attorney—who just happened to have been a civil engineer for the city some years earlier
- Securities attorney to keep QV legal
- Assortment of consultants, including engineers, surveyors, an environmental consultant
- CPA for accounting advice and filing necessary tax reports
- Cohousing development consultant—they chose CoHousing Solutions to guide them through the overall development process, particularly for budgeting, helping them apply for a construction loan, and selecting a building contractor
- Design architect—they chose Charles Durrett (McCamant & Durrett Architects) to work through the six design workshops, develop the strategy for obtaining permits, produce most of the construction documents and specifications, and finally, for construction quality control
- Local architect—they chose Richard Berg (Terrapin Architecture) to guide them through the process of obtaining entitlements and permits; Berg eventually served as the architect of record for finishing the construction drawings and specifications, and for routine construction administration
- General contractor—they chose Fairbank Construction Company
- Insurance broker for construction insurance, warranty, and liability insurance
- Consultant on governance, group process, decision-making (sociocracy), and dispute resolution (nonviolent communication)

In each case, QV entered into a written contract or agreement for services that clearly stated what work was to be done, by whom, when, and what the compensation would be. They were also sure to designate

The Role of a Cohousing Development Consultant

A cohousing development consultant played a key role in making Quimper Village a reality. CoHousing Solutions, operated by Katie McCamant, not only helped the group secure the construction loan for the project, she also participated in interviews of construction companies. Because of her long and successful track record in creating cohousing, she was able to provide credibility to any professionals who were skeptical about this thing called "cohousing." McCamant also provided unit costs, budgets, and more—tools that QV needed to confidently develop their project.

who took orders from whom and to whom they would report. QV tried to include a means of resolving disputes in each contract.

Forming the Finance & Legal Team

The first committee (team) QV established was Finance and Legal. Forming this team demonstrated the community's strong sense of responsibility and their desire to get this project going.

Let's repeat that. The FIRST team QV established was Finance and Legal. It wasn't Site Selection or Design or Landscaping or Green Living. It was old-fashioned, sort-of-intimidating, real-world-business. It was LEGAL and FINANCIAL.

For QV, the work of the Finance and Legal team included, but was not limited to:
- Retaining attorneys and a CPA
- Designing and drafting corporate legal documents: articles, bylaws, and so forth
- Handling purchases and sale of real estate
- Identifying a construction lender and managing the loan application process
- Creating and managing the budget
- Drafting and updating legal documents to meet federal and state securities regulations
- Developing and implementing a financing plan
- Negotiating and managing contracts with professionals, contractors, and others

The group.

- Drafting future owners' association documents
- Helping members obtain permanent financing
- Managing the closings on twenty-eight residential units

The team worked closely with their attorney on legal documents and used them for advice. They spoke frequently with the development consultant, primarily before construction started.

The legal structure was relatively easy to construct. QV created a cooperative association named Townsend Meadows Cooperative (TMC) and registered it with the state. Incorporation as an LLC (limited liability corporation) may be the appropriate legal entity for your state or province—be sure to find out. An LLC is created to do precisely as the name suggests, limit the financial liability of its members. QV drafted articles of incorporation and bylaws describing how people could become a member, designated

The landscapping was stark at the beginning, but now it's a whole new place.

all members as directors on the board of directors, selected officer positions, determined how they were going to make decisions, where the money was going to come from and go, and what would happen if they needed to terminate the organization.

Outlawed in Washington

Let's back up. When QV first created their LLC, it was called Quimper Village LLC. The members proceeded to go about marketing memberships. Flush with their pride and enthusiasm, they created bumper stickers, a website, and a newsletter, and they generated press coverage. Imagine their dismay (and shock) when they discovered what they were doing was illegal in Washington!

Why?

Because in the great state of Washington there are very strict rules around "what is being sold." While it seemed obvious to QV that "we were selling a way of life and a home to prospective members/residents,"

that is not how the U.S. Securities and Exchange Commission (SEC) saw it. Quimper Village had a problem. They had advertised all over the place that they were selling homes to prospective buyers. But in developing a cohousing community, as far as the SEC was concerned, they were not selling houses, because the houses hadn't been built yet. The SEC said that QV was selling their intention to build houses using other people's money. In particular, the people who became members of QV would be providing money for preconstruction activities. This was a problem because there was always the possibility that the project would not be completed and that all or part of the money would be lost. Under federal law, the QV group was selling a security. Since QV was developing their cohousing community in the State of Washington they were subject to Washington's securities regulations. The regulation that applied to their $10 + million project

> **A specialized attorney** (like a securities specialist) may charge more per hour than a general attorney, but just like a medical specialist there are similar benefits—more experience, quicker answers because they don't have to do lots of research on most things, and they are likely to have personal/professional contacts who can be very helpful.

limited them to marketing and selling their memberships only to persons whose primary residence was in Washington.

The leader of the QV Marketing Team had a number of difficult discussions with their securities attorney. Ultimately, all of their advertising materials (signs, newsletters, webpages, articles in magazines, and so on) were required to include information about this limitation.

So how did members discover they had been violating a state law? When they shared some of their early paperwork with a local attorney, this person recommended consulting a securities attorney. And then they got their big surprise. They then abandoned the Quimper Village LLC and created a new one, Townsend Meadows Cooperative.

U.S. Securities and Exchange Commission regulations require that all securities be registered with the SEC unless they are specifically exempted as a small offering by the state where the project is located. Some states, such as California, have very few regulations for small projects other than requiring that the seller provide a full disclosure of the risks involved. Other states (like Washington) have more complicated regulations that may restrict where, how, and to whom sales can be made.

The SEC episode cost the QV project a month of time, lots of effort, and many dollars to straighten out. The Washington-only ruling also meant that one couple from California had to leave the group. The Washington residency requirement may have been a blessing in disguise, though. Most of the members lived within two hours of Port Townsend, and so were able to attend the general membership meetings, social events, and participate on teams. This made integrating these out-of-town Washington folks into the community relatively easy to do. QV reported that it was harder to integrate members who lived farther away because they weren't able to participate on a regular basis.

It seems that all cohousing projects run into a few roadblocks. QV showed a remarkable ability

The Bylaws

Give some serious thought to the bylaws and their implications. Ask and answer the "what if" questions. They include:

Q: What happens to a member's money if they drop out?

A: There are many possible answers. QV agreed to refund as much of it as possible, plus 2 percent interest, when all development was completed. Prospective members will inevitably ask this question, so be prepared.

Q: If your intent is to be an owner-occupied community, what if someone becomes a member, closes on their unit, and then rents it out?

A: Answers vary. The point is you will need an answer to this question.

to assess their SEC problem and effectively address it. Staying in-state was effective for them—there were plenty of people right in their own backyard who wanted to live in their cohousing community, so that's where they focused their energy.

Most states require that an up-to-date disclosure document (Offering Memorandum)—which discloses all material facts, expectations, and risks of the project—be offered to any person who is considering purchasing a membership. QV created this document and made sure that all members signed an acknowledgement that they had received it. They even went a step further: a member of the Finance and Legal Team sat down with each prospective member and went through the document. QV found that thinking through all of this helped them organize and move forward in a very logical way, and it helped them educate prospective members about what they had done and what they planned to do. No one could later say, "You didn't tell me that." At the same time, it demonstrated that QV was not glossing over the details around this project.

QV's first Offering Memorandum was pretty slim. The final one was 127 pages long. It consisted of legal documents including the Articles of Incorporation, Bylaws, and the Declaration of Covenants, Conditions, and Restrictions (CC&Rs) of QV's condo owners association. The Offering Memorandum contained many warnings that a person could lose their money if they became a member before construction was completed. People joined anyway, because they were confident that QV members were thoughtful and thorough about what they were doing.

Lesson learned: Find out what your state's or province's regulations are and make sure you comply.

No Easy Outs: When Not to DIY

This legal and financial work seems like boring stuff. For sure it can be, especially when group members would rather be welcoming new folks and working on designs. But doing this vital work at the very beginning of the project will save time, effort, and money in the long run, and is part of getting the cool designs done.

By the same token, as the project progresses and expenses increase, it's tempting to look for ways to cut items from the budget. A group might say, "We'll save some money if we do it ourselves." This temptation is especially appealing when the group is faced with (yet another) decision about hiring (yet another) professional consultant, or when the project is under construction.

In QV's experience, "doing it ourselves" usually cost them more money, took longer, and was a lot more work. The results were often worse too. Think carefully before succumbing to that temptation.

For example, QV did not contract with a landscape architect. They relied instead on a member with some background in landscape design. In other words, they tried to save money by not professionally designing and installing the landscape, plus they figured they could do it later. But this was a shortsighted move in retrospect. With a six-acre plot of land there was a lot of landscaping to be designed and installed. Walkways, patios, fencing, trees, grass, gravel, and more all had to be dealt with. Most importantly, swales needed to be created. A professional landscape designer would have assisted the group in addressing these issues, and may have found other things thay they weren't aware of. The bottom line was this: QV did not save money on their landscaping. In fact, a year after move-in they were still struggling with basics of their extensive landscape. It also distracted their other consultants (the architect and civil engineer, in particular), because they did not have reliable, professional information to do their work. This meant that they had to fill in the gaps themselves.

Lesson learned: Use the expertise of the people in your community to interface with the professionals, but not to do the actual work.

Residents settling in. Now there is life between the buildings.

An Interview with Katie McCamant
Development Consultant, CoHousing Solutions

Alexandria: What is your connection with cohousing?

Katie: I first came across cohousing as an architecture student in Copenhagen, the same year I met Chuck Durrett there. It seemed like such an obvious solution to building neighborhoods that addressed the changing demographics of family life. I was shocked when I got to UC Berkeley the next year, and no one had heard of it. Along with publishing our first book on cohousing in 1988, Chuck and I established our architecture firm. In addition to providing architectural services to cohousing groups, I found a need for project management. It was critical to figure out the development budgets, financing and investment mechanisms, and all the other aspects of getting projects built. Over the last three decades I have worked as an architect, project manager, developer, and consultant for cohousing communities, as well as living in my own communities through all the different stages of my life.

Alexandria: How does a Development Consultant work with a cohousing group?

Katie: My goal with CoHousing Solutions is to help new communities build on the best practices we've refined over the last three decades of collaborative development experience, and assist each community in figuring out how to put together an effective professional team and strategy for their specific situation. I am often the first consultant a community hires, so I start by exploring what they have in place. Do they have a marketing and membership process? Do they need to build awareness of what cohousing offers to get others thinking about why they might want to buy into a community? Can they raise the financial resources to purchase property? Who are the other key consultants they'll need? Is there a developer they might partner with? I build a development budget to help them get real about what it will cost and put together a path forward.

Alexandria: What is your process, what are your goals, and how did you assist QV specifically?

Katie: I worked closely with QV to put together and refine a realistic development budget. I also worked on how to control their costs. Once they had their design, we put together a package to explore construction financing with several local banks. Then we selected a general contractor. That effort really paid off when we were able to get very competitive fees from both the construction lender and general contractor. Both were impressed by how disciplined the community was and their understanding of the role they needed to play in holding costs.

Alexandria: It seems like QV came together more quickly than many other cohousing projects. What do you attribute that to?

Katie: QV benefitted from starting with a strong group of initial households, many of which already knew each other from the local Unitarian Church. That founding group had many skills within it, as well as financial resources. Since many were retired, they were able to dedicate significant time to the effort.

QV was able to secure excellent terms for construction financing from a local bank without a development partner. That was a combination of a strong project, but also some luck and good timing. I have found that many projects benefit from partnering with a professional developer, particularly more complex urban communities. Each situation is different and the trick is figuring out the best development strategy for a specific community, and its time and place.

QV is a great community. But if we want to make collaborative neighborhoods available to a greater number of people, if we want to scale cohousing, we'll need more professionals that know how to work in a collaborative development process. That is why I started the 500 Communities Training, to train the next generation of professionals to work with communities like this. We can build on the best practices these communities have refined, but we'll also need people who can adapt these ideas to the future needs of our ever-changing world. I'm excited to see how the movement grows and adapts in the next decades.

6

"The aim of argument, or of discussion, should not be victory, but progress."
— *Joseph Joubert*

Dynamic What?

QUIMPER VILLAGE GOT OFF to a terrific start, in large part because they were aware that they would need a highly functioning system of governance and structured decision making. As QV said, "Your community will have a governance system . . . why not be deliberate about what it is?"

Very early in the life of most cohousing communities, the members develop a values statement that guides them in developing and living in their community. Most of these statements say something about living sustainably, building connections, and honoring and respecting all ideas. That last one can be translated to mean that every member has an equal voice in what happens in the community and that, since all are bound by group decisions, every member should be willing to abide by the decision.

QV quickly agreed that the standard meeting procedures detailed in *Robert's Rules of Order* results in winners and losers. Such outcomes did not bode well for community living. They also agreed that out of respect for everyone's time, energy, and intellect, meetings should be well planned, time spent on them should be economical, and they should result in decisions that all members could at least tolerate, if not approve of.

Pat Hundhausen discovered the concept of dynamic governance, otherwise known as sociocracy, by reading the book "We the People" by John Buck and Sharon Villines, and from other resources. Sociocracy seemed to be a good anecdote to majority rule and consensus, the frequent alternative. As luck would have it, a course on nonviolent communication was in

Values Statement

All cohousing groups come up with a mission and values statement, or a vision statement. This is QV's statement, which they started during their Getting-It-Built Workshop and refined later. Interestingly, many of those who helped create this statement did not end up in the community. Still, it worked to get them through development.

We believe community relationships and caring attitudes create vibrant lives that enrich our health and well-being, while encouraging enthusiasm, humor, joy, patience, flexibility, and mutual respect.

We honor the natural attributes of our physical site and its surrounding environment.

We seek to find economical and sustainable practices that meet our needs.

We value a balance of quality and economy with beauty and convenience that appeals to the broadest spectrum of the community.

We are an intentional community that honors and respects all ideas. Through gathering information and by thoughtful evaluation we come to consensus (agreement). We strive to find balance between individual interests and the greater good of our community.

We value and respect the wisdom that comes from lifelong experiences.

An Interview with Araya Sol
By Chuck Durrett

Chuck: What qualities do you think people should have or need to foster in order to participate in cohousing?

Araya: I think definitely cooperation—that's the most important. And understanding. I think those are the two most important. Also be willing to work. I mean, this is not easy. And I think that's why a lot of people shy away from cohousing. It's because they don't want to work so hard. They're more willing to pay a manager to do it.

progress at their UU Fellowship church. The facilitator, Alex Bryan, also consulted on dynamic governance. The cohousing group hired Bryan to teach them how to organize and facilitate their meetings, how to make decisions, and how to select members for specific positions.

I initially was on marketing, but it was inspiring and intriguing to me to consider consensus and then sociocracy. The whole momentum of being able to work on two levels, one as a participant, the other as a facilitator, and to guide proposals and discussions, has turned out to be a lot of fun... We just jumped in and took off. I was simply intrigued by both guiding a group through a process to help us reach our potential and for personal growth.
—Janet Palmer

A principle of sociocracy is the idea of consent. This is different than consensus, which operates on the principle that everyone must agree. In consent decision-making, everyone agrees that a decision is "within one's range of tolerance." Along the way the group works to hear opinioned voices as it fashions a proposal that can fall within their range of tolerance. Proposals include a sunset clause so that they can be revisited, which further reduces the pressure on agreement. It's "good enough for now, safe enough to try." The only reason to vote against something is if it is dangerous or is seriously against the mission and values of the community.

The sociocracy process for elections is remarkable. They start off with: You don't let anyone volunteer. You just go around and everyone's supposed to say who they think ought to get a duty and why. And the person is not allowed to say, "No, I don't want it." So then you make the rounds, and quite often by mechanisms that are not clear to me, sometimes it takes a couple passes. But then the people tend to sort of glom on to one person and the person has not yet said they're willing to do it. However, what the person has heard everyone in the group saying is, "We think you ought to do it and we'll be supportive of that." And so it's kind of hard to turn down at that point. The other big conceptual change for people is that we do consent decision-making rather than consensus. In other words, is something within your range of tolerance? And that is so remarkably different from majority rule. It's just worlds different and really smart.

—Mark Sloan

There are lots of resources available to learn more about dynamic governance and its many varieties, but in a nutshell, it is a process that helps a group move forward on challenging decisions. It allows groups to focus not on people's individual preferences, but where they find common ground. When working with more than thirty people to design a housing community, this concept can be very useful. A group can and should hire someone trained in this skill to teach them how to use it, and to get them on the road to making decisions in this way. That said, QV did all of the design workshops with Chuck by consensus. Although not everyone spoke on each line item, Chuck helped to garner information from each and every person who had new and compelling arguments. Chuck has a lot of skill and experience at helping a group reach their potential quickly through consensus, but QV did all other non-design work using sociocracy. Most cohousing projects in the world have been created by consensus. Experience is what makes consensus work.

Jerry didn't know if he'd like cohousing, but he's usually the life of the party.

An Interview with Jerry Spieckerman
By Chuck Durrett and Alexandria Levitt

Jerry: And then it hit me. "Yes, I want friends when I grow older." I've been here a year and a half now. What I enjoy the most is that our house is very central.

What I found to be the most desirable thing is when it gets warmer I can sit out on my porch. If I go at nine o'clock after breakfast, I will not be alone on my porch until after lunch. I'm so glad that I can sit out there for a couple hours. People keep coming by. That's one of the highlights of living here to me. It's unbelievable.

Alexandria: There's a lot you enjoy here, but are there things you find challenging about living here?

Jerry: You don't necessarily get along with everybody. One of my fears of moving here was that I would piss in somebody's cornflakes and they'd be mad at me.

That's my personality. One of the things I found is because of the amount of activity I've done here and continue to do I get a lot of respect from people because of that, which I find very satisfying.

Chuck: Yes. So in a way, Jerry, what you've just said is that you know getting along with everyone is the number one challenge of living in cohousing. The currency of cohousing is if you do work, you gain respect. This helps mitigate the ruffled feathers. But are there other ways that you help mitigate ruffled feathers? In other words, have you evolved? Have you changed living here?

Jerry: Oh, yes. I've tried to mellow out and to accept the fact that not all my ideas are the best ideas. I can live with that. There's a lot going on here that I wouldn't do, and that's just fine. Back to your original question. Yes, I'm a can-doer and you'll find there's lots to do here. You can take on projects and continue to do things to satisfy that need.

7

"Do you love life? If so, then do not squander time, because that's the stuff life is made of."
— *Olawale Daniel*

Time Is Money

THE REAL SECRET WAS that everybody started to pay from day one. Everybody had their money in the game, and everybody had the same level of commitment. Every two months we had to pay five thousand dollars. Carrying costs. They were to service the land every month, among other things. In the end, everybody had thirty-five thousand dollars in our account.

— *Jerry Spieckerman*

It's one thing to have the funds on hand for coffee and pastries to offer at a meeting in a church classroom or someone's home. It's quite another to hire architects and engineers and be in charge of building a $10 million neighborhood. To most people, that seems pretty daunting, if not impossible. How much help is needed? From whom? When? How? What will it cost? If a cohousing project is to become real, however, everyone in the group will need to make a serious financial contribution. Once costs for the project are established, a schedule of payments can be set up and implemented, creating a roadmap to reach the financial goals. It's that opportunity to put hard money into a project that demonstrates who is serious about living in a cohousing community.

It is inherently speculative. You are putting money on the line and trusting the other people in the group who, together, are going to pull this off, and that's tremendously risky. You can't have your own personal preferences and bulldoze the group, because it's not going to flow. You're merging your preferences, and you have to be willing to give something up if it doesn't work for everybody, and it doesn't matter how much money you have because it's not going to happen. It has to balance out, and you want the development to be as economical as it can be because there are people who have less, and you don't want to push them away by forcing your decisions on the full group. So it's give and take. I was in.

—Janet Palmer

In the beginning, QV started small. Each person put in $25 when needed to help cover meeting space rentals, copying, the website, and other small expenses. When they decided to proceed with the project, the founding members established a membership fee of $500 per household. This paid early legal and development consulting fees. When QV found the land and started preconstruction work, they needed significantly more money. They worked with their development consultant to create the initial preconstruction budget and expenditure timeline so they could project how much money was needed and when.

Financing Plan

Townsend Meadows Cooperative (TMC) raised the money for the project from three sources.

The members of TMC provided the money for preconstruction development expenses.

The land seller accepted a TMC mortgage for most of the land purchase. They paid $25,000 down and the seller agreed to an interest-only repayment schedule until the project was completed and all the other debts were paid off.

An Interview with Carolyn Salmon

By Chuck Durrett and Alexandria Levitt

Carolyn: You know, the budget and the timeline that Katie (McCamant) put together provides a way so you can see where you need to go, and when you have to, and in this period we're going to be doing this and it's going to cost us this much. Now let's move to getting that done. And now what do we do to have that money that we need? Right. So we've got it in hand and everybody made their payments on time. We never had anybody that we had to go back and say, "Hey you haven't paid your money." That's part of it, of course, looking at their assets and cash availability.

Alexandria: But it also sounds like, Carolyn, that part of your role was sitting down with people and walking them through it or just being sure. So you're saying, "We have five households. I'm not saying who they are but they're on the edge. So we need to keep this budget tight because they might not feel comfortable saying so themselves." So you're very discreet and calm, and it seems like that would serve the process well.

Carolyn: I think it did. I think we were able to stay right on the line and be reassuring to those folks that were really trying.

Alexandria: That takes a lot of confidence for me to come to you and say, "These are my personal finances. There you go." And then you say, "That looks great, I think it's going to be fine, or I'm a little concerned."

Carolyn: Did you really think about this? And whether you can take this risk.

Chuck: Because that's subjective. Some people can take the risk but don't think they can, and some people can't and think they can.

> **Condominium vs. Cohousing**
>
> If the final form of ownership is a condominium, use the term "condominium" instead of "cohousing" when talking to the bank and general contractors. "Condominium" is a word they know and understand, and this word will increase their comfort level with a proposed project.

With the property in place, TMC obtained a commercial construction loan on the strength of their combined assets and borrowing power.

Prospective new residents who came into the project paid a $500 application fee. This became their membership fee if they stayed on and actually joined the community. Each prospective resident was asked to provide a financial statement and a prequalification approval letter from a mortgage lender for an 80 percent mortgage for the estimated price of the particular unit they planned to buy. These documents were reviewed by the Finance Team, a member of which had extensive experience in financial planning. If someone did not seem to have adequate income or assets, a Finance Team member had the difficult conversation with them about these concerns. As she said, "We did not want someone losing money that could affect their ability to live a comfortable life in the future or to not be able to close when the project was completed."

Again the members of QV showed that they had an extraordinary attention to detail and a willingness to deal with the difficult issues right away (for example, asking people, "Can you really afford this?"). This proactive approach saved them all time and money in the end.

The future residents of QV were also faced with a significant challenge around this time when two member families pulled out of the project. Their exit left the group feeling a mix

Light and airy houses.

of emotions, but Pat didn't panic. She grabbed the reigns and created a plan to keep the group on track and on the critical path. She drafted a letter to all of the remaining residents (which can be seen in Appendix C), that reassured the community that they would persevere.

QV created an incentive program where people who put their money in early were rewarded by getting a discount on the price of their house, and at the front of the line when it came time to choose their unit. These discounts were built into overall costs.

QV established a system they called Required Capital Contributions (RCC). In essence, this created a timeline of payments from the members that would keep the project moving. This was also a great way to link payment to outcomes. Folks joining later in the process paid the cumulative RCCs that existing members had already made. Every household had the same financial commitment during preconstruction work.

Just prior to closing on the construction loan, each household paid the remainder of the amount needed to bring the member contribution up to 22 percent of the base price of their house. The bank required 20 percent. QV chose 22 percent because this gave them more cash on hand for the preconstruction costs. Since the construction loan only covered actual general contractor construction costs, TMC, as the developer, was responsible

Affordability

QV did not include affordable housing units in their project. There were no local or state funds available (it's a city by city policy) and the members did not feel they could personally underwrite affordable units. In a perfect world, there would be a way to do this with affordable units, but QV made a decision based on expediency and what they could afford. This made the reality check on members' finances early on even more important.

QV was motivated to control costs so that middle income people who had signed on could stay on. Five future residents, having obtained prequalification letters and the Finance Team's approval, were still on the edge financially. QV kept them in by staying prudent about costs. MDA Architects had a sense of how many households were in this position and was motivated to keep them in the deal. It was important to the QV group in general, and the Finance Team in particular, to keep costs at a level so all fully committed members could remain part of the project. One of the best ways to keep a cohousing project affordable is to get people involved from the beginning that truly need it to be affordable. Since no one in the group wanst to lose them, they will do whatever they can to keep them in, including controling costs.

People are too often sure that clustered housing will have less light inside. You get what you design—just like a car, just like a phone, just like a house.

for paying for all preconstruction costs, operating expenses for the organization, and any development costs that were not in the general contractor's contract. By having adequate cash on hand, they had the cash they needed when they needed it, and they were able to save on interest payments to the bank. As a successful developer, TMC completed the project with cash in the bank. They used some of it to pay for some particularly desirable extras for the community, and they provided a return of capital to all members. They also refunded the households that had dropped out of the project, plus 2 percent interest.

Other sources of development funding for a cohousing project can include loans from members or investors. These loans could be interest bearing and/or could include some participation in any "profit" on the project.

Budget

After the initial design work was done, the cohousing development

Why People Leave a Cohousing Project

People drop out of cohousing projects at many stages along the way, including:
- Affordability
- Personal circumstances/choice/ a job out of town
- The payment of a significant membership fee
- Spouse's choice
- Down payment requirement
- A closer look at their own finances

While it is easy to panic when this happens, it should be viewed as a natural process of finding the right members. There are many points along the way when the project gets "real" to people—finding a site, paying a significant cost to join, making a down payment, and more. Sometimes a spouse finds they just can't do it, or a person realizes it is not for them when they closely examine their finances. It is better to lose people who are not on board than to try to hang on to them at any cost. This opens up the membership to other people who can participate enthusiastically and without hesitation.

consultant, Katie McCamant, put together some initial price ranges for each unit.

- 2 bedroom/1 bath, 910 square feet: $277,000–$297,000
- 2 bed/2 bath, 1,195 square feet: $370,000–390,000
- 3 bed/2 bath, 1,335 square feet: $405,000–$425,000

These estimates established some realistic cost figures, which allowed potential members to determine whether or not they could afford to join. Using those figures, plus the cost of various line items based on the experience of recently constructed cohousing communities and the actual costs of some items, McCamant built the initial budget for the project. This budget was constantly revised as new information was gathered.

QV's change orders for construction came to about 3.5 percent of the contracted total cost of construction. (A change order is work that is added to or deleted from the original scope of work of a contract. However, depending on the magnitude of the change, it may or may not alter the original contract amount and/or completion date. Ultimately, change orders may force a project to handle, sometimes, significant changes and should be approached with restraint or be avoided altogether.) Remembering that time is money, QV focused on keeping their project moving. They

The entrance to the common house. Lots of light!

assumed any changes and delays would increase costs.

Final construction costs for QV came in below the adjusted total cost of construction (costs including change orders). QV split the savings 50/50 with their general contractor.

Construction Loan

QV submitted applications to five banks while searching for a construction loan. In the end, they selected a smaller, regional bank called First Federal. They got to know their loan officer well, and they kept the bank informed about the progress with their planning approvals even before they made their formal application for a construction loan, and of course they kept the bank informed throughout construction. It was valuable to have McCamant meet with the team that handled the bank loan, especially since QV was operating as their own developer.

McCamant was able to provide credibility about cohousing and explain how other lenders had approached cohousing loans. She could translate the needs and structure of a cohousing community to a lender who was unfamiliar with this concept. This helped cement the construction loan.

QV had sold twenty-three of the twenty-eight memberships when they closed on the construction loan. The bank offered a loan of 80 percent of the construction cost at prime plus 1 percent interest rate with closing costs of about $70,000 for the entire $10 million dollar loan. Each member household had to provide a guarantee for the base price of their house. That is, if the project tanked, individuals would pay the outstanding balance depending on where they were in the process.

QV started construction on July 25, 2016, with four unsold units. Three of these units sold within forty-five days and the last unit sold in February of 2017.

To get this done, QV recruited middle income folks who had steady income and adequate assets to purchase a home and live in it long term. The final base prices of their units ranged from $297,000 to $425,000. Upgrades, options, and appliances were extra. Some examples of upgrades and options were flooring and countertops that were not agreed upon by QV as a whole, extra outlets, wall and ceiling dimmers, and appliances.

Total member equity in the project was just over $2,000,000, and all of it was at risk if QV was not able to complete the project. After each completed day of construction, the Finance Team felt that cloud of risk lifting.

It's worth noting that the lender of the construction loan expected all the units to be "sold" at market rate. The difference between the total market prices and the costs of development and construction was the "profit."

Separated houses don't promote a feeling of community and connection, but these do.

8

"It is good people who make good places."
— *Anna Sewell,* **Black Beauty**

Finding and Purchasing Six Acres

BESIDES HELPING TO DESIGN what their new home will look like, finding a location is what excites most cohousers. It's also one of the most challenging parts of the process. Countless groups have washed up and washed out on these treacherous shoals. Why? There are a number of reasons, all of which QV deftly avoided.

In many cases, people are unrealistic about what they can find. In some parts of the country (especially urban areas) finding six acres like QV did is mostly a dream. It's important to note that most cohousing projects are on much smaller sites. For example, Walnut Commons in Santa Cruz, California, has 19 units on 0.24 acres. PDX Commons in Portland, Oregon, has 27 units on 0.4 acres.

People tend to get caught up in a fantasy of where they want to live (by the beach, in the best neighborhoods, and the like). As a result, they overlook a perfectly suitable piece of property in a transitioning part of town.

Groups that aren't well organized will have neither the money nor the organizational structure to put in an offer when something does come along.

Sites may have flaws that cohousing groups see as being insurmountable. These flaws, for example, could be excessive grading or toxic cleanup. An experienced developer, however, knows which problems can be overcome.

Putting in an offer for a piece of property is not difficult, but there are a lot of tricks of the trade and to most cohousing groups this is new territory. How did QV overcome this hurdle and end up with a special place? The first thing the initial members did was establish some criteria for the site they wanted. Ideally their site would be:

- About four acres, so they would have room for single-story buildings
- In town, so they could access public water and sewer
- Fairly level, so it would be easier to build on and would be easily navigable as the residents got older
- Close enough to walk to some shopping
- Close to a bus line
- Have good air quality that was not affected by a nearby paper mill

Cohousing is the antidote to boxes spread out across the landscape. Cohousing is the reintroduction to the village.

One member reviewed all vacant properties on the market against their criteria. She then identified all vacant multiple acre parcels on a detailed map of the city so as to determine which, if any, were on the market. She compared these properties to their criteria.

If a vacant parcel did match their criteria and was not on the market, she contacted the owner (getting this contact information was as simple as reviewing county tax records). She described the project and asked the owner if they would consider selling it. If so, she asked what the asking price might be. Ultimately, she identified eight pieces of property that met some of the criteria with potentially willing sellers. The sites ranged in size from a square block (great location) to a two-acre site (supportive realtor) with a house and several outbuildings that might be retrofitted.

QV organized a field trip to visit each of the properties. Each member was asked to rate the sites on the criteria, along with any comments. Three or four sites were quickly eliminated—too far out, not large enough, unappealing neighborhood. The city block they looked at was owned by a family whose son was an architect. He liked QV's story and did a mini-design workshop to show how QV could build multistory buildings on the site. Ultimately, his family decided they didn't want to sell, which worked out since QV had decided they did not want a multistory project. QV preferred the concept of one-story cottages tied together by meandering walkways, and they were fortunate to be in a part of the country where there were land options to support that preference.

David and Chuck planning the site.

QV narrowed down the field to two sites, the six-acre site they ultimately purchased, and a four-acre rolling site about half a mile to the west. More research showed that the four-acre site could present difficulties reaching the sewer line. It may have needed a pump station, and it would have be a tight fit for 25–28 homes, garages, and parking. Durrett and McCamant looked at

A group picnic on the site.

the two sites and recommended the six-acre parcel.

The site is oddly shaped. It features a long narrow entry that required QV to build a city street—an obstacle, but one they could overcome. Durrett and McCamant suggested QV obtain options from both sellers to give them time to do the due diligence they needed—discuss each parcel with the city planning department to find out what they would require, perform soil sampling tests, obtain estimates on the cost of likely site development requirements, engage in a Phase 1 Environmental Site Assessment, and so forth.

The options asked for 180 days to conduct due diligence and included purchase terms. The terms for the six-acre property was a purchase price of $500,000 with a $25,000 earnest money deposit (refundable within 180 days) to be applied to purchase at closing. The seller had stipulated that at least 25 percent of the total acreage of the property be retained as open space in one contiguous piece of land, as he wanted to preserve its natural beauty.

QV subsequently negotiated with the seller that he would carry a mortgage of $474,000 at 5 percent interest. The mortgage was to be paid off within 60 days of Quimper Village obtaining a construction loan. As that time approached, QV asked the seller to "subjugate his mortgage to the construction loan for an increase in interest to 6 percent." Quimper Village members were concerned he might not agree and that they would have to come up with the $474,000 outright. The Finance and Legal Team were quietly talking to some members and possible outside investors about loans. Fortunately they didn't have to do that. The seller carried the land

The vision.

Starting Off on the Right Foot with the Neighbors

A thought on after you have your land

by **Pam Clise**

In the process of creating Quimper Village, a neighborhood of seniors, we also created a larger neighborhood with the neighbors in the homes surrounding our property and across the valley.

We connected with that wider neighborhood as soon as we began our planning in October 2014. We went house to house to the neighbors of our then vacant property and/or wrote letters inviting them to comment on early plans so that we could understand their concerns. We went on to address those concerns through our process of creating the plans. We continued to offer avenues of communication by designating two contact points, so that we were able to address issues that might come up as we moved earth and began to do the hammering and nailing part of the project. We put MDA drawings up along the construction fencing that showed the overall plan to keep them informed. There were occasional disruptions in the flow of an otherwise peaceful process, yet our hope was always to make those interruptions short in order to get back to the business of just being good neighbors. As we finished our project, we followed up with thank you notes to neighbors for their patience and communications along the way, inviting them all to our first open house.

While listening and responding to neighbors beyond our borders, we found ourselves expanding our own understanding of what it means to live in this valley, and what it means to us all.

The common vision of a healthy life between the buildings.

A street view of QV's common house. This area is frequently the hub of activity.

mortgage, which means QV did not need to pay the land costs until the project was complete, and the houses were sold.

There is some secret sauce in this story. The couple who spoke with the property owner had significant experience in this area and were excellent negotiators. They scored an incredible price for the property and obtained an extremely generous agreement to subjugate the mortgage. Not everyone can accomplish that.

Another wrinkle in this is that Durrett told QV from the start that their property was in a low area, and for the purpose of proper drainage would need massive amounts of dirt to regrade it. It came as a surprise to QV when they realized they would have to spend an extra $300,000 on dirt. This additional cost to their budget raised concerns about selling all their units. In the end it worked out, but this wrinkle is an important reminder that pretty much all projects face significant, unforeseen hurdles.

There is much more to obtaining a site than described here. Local governments require numerous approvals in order for a group to proceed with a project. Expert help is critical with this. Ideally, this help comes from multiple sources: a local architect who knows the local commissioners and officials; an out-of-town architect who is experienced in cohousing and who knows what other cohousing projects have been able to negotiate; a local lawyer with relevant local experience; and someone who knows how the local planning department works and what their expectations are. All this said, it turned out beneficial to have

an out-of-town architect. Cohousing is always different, that is new and improved, anyway. Someone has to know how to prove that, and local officials are always worried about new ideas. Local architects usually say yes to everything that bureaucrats demand, when it's usually not necessary, usually more costly, and too often extremely deleterious to cohousing. I can take you to several cohousing kitchens that no one wants to cook in. And the people hours, therefore, in the common house, are 150 instead of 350 which is where it would be if done well. The bad kitchens were more expensive to build, but at the end of the process, no one wanted to be there. There are too many examples like this in cohousing, where too much money is spent to make the environment worse.

Moreover, there is customarily some kind of public hearing process where future neighbors will tell the hearing officials how wonderful the project is but how awful it is for their neighborhood. QV tried to ameliorate this pushback by making personal contact with as many of the nearby neighbors as possible, and by sending them frequent emails about what they were doing. This public hearing process typically takes longer than a group might anticipate and can be more aggravating than necessary. It took QV seven months to complete the public hearing process. But they did it!

McCamant & Durrett Architects almost always suggest a planned unit development (PUD) application, and QV was no exception. A PUD means that whatever the zoning code says about numerous things, from parking space requirements to color selection, you don't have to go in that direction if there's a better way. In essence, a PUD means that you need to propose something better than the zoning code, and that's always easy to do and garners flexibility. Also, in many cases, these proposals end up saving considerable costs for the project.

All day Saturday and Sunday, then from 6—9 pm on Monday and Tuesday, twelve site plans were produced — a record number. This one was agreed upon because it best reflected the goals, activities, places, and behaviors that they hoped to achieve.

9

"First life, then spaces, then buildings —The other way around never works."
— Jan Gehl.

The Design of Quimper Village

THE DESIGN PROCESS IS when a unique collection of people, both individually and collectively, express their aspirations and find out who they want to become.

One of the priorities of the community design is to preserve, facilitate, and enhance the richness of life there long after the "honeymoon" has worn off. One could argue that the primary responsibility of the design process is the product. True, but the product of consequence is a collection of people who know how to stitch together a place of consequence. They build the place, not brick by brick but decision by decision, and one healthy relationship at a time. After the Getting-It-Built Workshop, the QV group scheduled seven design workshops with McCamant and Durrett Architects.

Durrett says, "In the context of designing new senior cohousing communities, no one ever said, 'Give me a vanilla suburban subdivision,' though many of them might have lived in that world at one point. It seemed like they knew that they wanted something vastly different—but what exactly? The design workshops gave them the opportunity to discover that for themselves."

This process is essential in that it creates the design of a given cohousing community while forging the relationships among the residents that will get a pro-social, and adequately private environment built. For that, a process of discussion and discovery has to happen. In QV's case, these workshops were to take place over five to six months. The participatory design process has many moving

Quimper Village: the synthesis of the common visions.

parts and juggles varying ideas. And the best design for that community emerges from it. The process is extremely rewarding and has its lighter moments too. The result is a high-functioning neighborhood where the collective and individual lives of the community are made easier, more practical, more convenient, more economical, and more fun."

The future residents of QV wondered, "What will my house look like? How much will it cost?" Through Durrett's deliberate interactive sessions, the design, estimated costs of the site, common house, and individual homes were clarified. But he was always working backwards from what the bank said each of these residents could afford. A hugely important consequence of working through the design workshops is that it binds a group together with a good working knowledge of a consensus-based decision-making process. In the case of QV, they successfully wove together their unified preferences and tolerances while staying focused on the critical path.

Design Workshop 1: Site Plan Program and Schematic Design

The first design workshop for QV began in September 2014. The group spent two days creating design criteria, and two evenings creating a site plan. They addressed the site design program first, because the design of the site would largely determine the type of social environment within QV and make predicting a budget much easier. The result of Design Workshop 1 was a preliminary site plan that showed the location of the homes, garages, common house, outbuildings, auxiliary parking, gardens, gathering areas, and more.

To get to that point, QV first discussed their aspirations for the project. In general, they were looking for a design that complemented their value statement. Qualities they wanted (in their own words) included the following: connection, friends are there, no visible cars, combination of privacy and community, close proximity,

Site designing with clear criteria is extremely gratifying and productive. Working without it is frustrating. QV spent two days defining what they wanted before starting the process.

In the American suburb, the normal distance from doorknob to doorknob is 110 feet. The QV group started 110 feet apart and were asked to walk towards each other and when one person stopped, so did the other. The distance between each person would eventually be the distance between their front doors. They ended at 15 to 33 feet apart.

colorful, inclusion, walkability with accessibility, physical and emotional safety, feel proud, "was worth it," "we did it together," feeling of "vision," and ecologically appropriate. Activities they wanted included: dancing, yoga, bocce ball, watching sunsets and stars, wheelchair racing, sitting and chatting in small groups, gardening, and charging autos. Places included: garden, open space, front porch, common terrace, storage, hanging clothes, gathering places, parking lot, and outdoor workspaces.

To create the site plan, QV broke up into two groups (no spouses together) to talk about what layout would fulfill their criteria. Each group came up with a plan for the village using wooden blocks to signify buildings, and cardboard to signify grass and walkways. Durrett critiqued them and then the two groups coalesced with a final plan.

At the end of Sunday, Durrett led the QV residents in an exercise to determine how far apart their front doors should be from each other. He had them think in terms of creating a site plan based on caring about each other. And since they had done so much work together by now, they knew what he meant. "Imagine you had dinner with a neighbor last night, say Sunday evening. She had indicated that she was going to have a very difficult conversation with an adult child later that evening, for example about a divorce, or a death in the family. Now imagine that it's 8:30 the next morning and you are both opening your front doors at the same time. You don't want to pry, but you do care, and may want to contact her later, and would at least like to see what kind of a mood she is in.

Now I want you to walk towards each other until one of you stops—then I want you both to stop. That's what the distance will be from front doorknob to front doorknob. If anyone doesn't want the distance to be closer than 110 feet, then neither of you move at all."

The group determined from that exercise that, for them, the ideal distance between front doors was 15–33 feet. And when the neighborhood was eventually built, they were set within this range.

Design Workshop 2: Common House Program and Schematic Design

One month after Design Workshop 1 was complete, the group did two days of programming for the common house in Design Workshop 2. This workshop established the goals and priorities for common facilities, and detailed the specific activities that would take place there. The purpose of this workshop was not to design the common house itself, but rather to establish specific guidelines that would be used for the basis of the design. Put another way, this workshop established the design criteria for the individual spaces within the building. To accomplish this, QV needed to fully comprehend the needs, wants, and desires of their group. It was literally an anthropological act. A guiding question was, "Who are we and who do we want to be, and how will the common facilities facilitate both of these?"

QV began by making a list of activities and goals for the common house and then putting them up on a wall where they were discussed and refined. Some of the goals for the common house included manifesting the community they developed, inviting, easy to maintain, good acoustics, natural light, and supporting of health. Activities included eating together, sitting by the fire, conversing, doing laundry, and hosting guests. QV had the chance to think about how these intentions would manifest, and with that in mind they prioritized what mattered most.

This conversation also covered what common activities would happen outside the common house, or which features they would place outside (an art studio, for example), and what spaces would be inside the common house (a dining room, kitchen, living room, guest rooms, caregiver suite, laundry room, mailboxes, and a foyer). For cost reasons, QV decided ultimately to locate their woodworking shop, bicycle barn, and art studio in the garage buildings.

Durrett reminded the group that if the common house was done right, the smaller private residences would have over 4,000 square feet of amenities available to them. In other

One of three groups of QV residents working together to decide what rooms they wanted to include in their common house design.

The final common house design. It included guest rooms and a caretaker apartment.

Residents improving the common house design.

words, a 1,000-square-foot house would effectively be a 5,000-square-foot house. That is, the common house would supplement the needs of the private houses, and at the same time, foster the community. Because the common house had guest rooms, the private houses could be smaller.

Design Workshop 2 was a lot of fun. It was a fantastic community building experience because it revealed the residents' commonalities and their goals for the future. The completed common house is used every day. QV recently computed the people-hours for a typical week. They found that their common house was used for 366.5 people hours per week, which is an above average number.

Design Workshop 3: Private House Program and Schematic Design

A month after Design Workshop 2, QV members participated in Design Workshop 3. In this workshop they considered the design of the individual homes. Durrett worked with the group to decide the private house sizes, room-by-room requirements, and the design. The members chose to have three unit designs:

- 2 bedroom/1 bath at 910 square feet (12 units)
- 2 bedroom/2 bath at 1,195 square feet (8 units)
- 3 bedroom/2 bath at 1,335 square feet (8 units)

Durrett began with a basic floor plan that he had sketched up based on their budget, site, and common house design. Over three days, QV worked to perfect the design. Durrett met with the residents of each unit type to consider possible changes to the floor plans and to come to agreement concerning the design. Because the residents already understood how the large common house fit into the overall design of the community, they were prepared to allow their individual homes to be smaller and more efficient. For example, because common laundry facilities were located in the common house, the individual homes did not necessarily need to have a laundry area.

QV's goals for the private homes included spaciousness, clean lines, natural lighting, uncluttered atmosphere, no wasted space, cozy, and no sound transmission through the shared walls. Activities included private time, cooking, sleeping (of course), and sharing a pot of coffee with a neighbor on a whim. Spaces included private house decks, storage, kitchen, and a living room. In Design Workshop 3, QV members became comfortable with and enthusiastic about this new downsized idea of "home." They discovered that they could retain what they loved most in their private homes, while placing them in the larger context of the village they were creating.

The design of the private homes was done in the context of the design of the common house. The members embraced the common house as a major amenity to each private house, viewing it as a supplement, even an extension. Again, intentional design can be a bit of an anthropological exercise, and Quimper Village residents grasped their intentions entirely.

Keep what we love (our home), lose what we don't love (our clutter), and marry them to a new view. The window above the kitchen sink is where you can watch the world pass by, knowing that the common house has guest rooms and more. This knowledge makes it easier for people to envision living in a smaller private space.

The A-building home types (two bedroom, one bath), the B-types (two bedroom, two baths), and the C-types (three bedroom, two baths) were designed separately. But, together they fit into the context of a custom neighborhood where the sum is greater than the parts.

Design Workshop 4: Design Closure Workshop

At QV's fourth workshop (the Design Closure Workshop) the design was presented in the context

The environmentalist of the future is the acoustic engineer in concert with his/her architect practitioner/collaborator. Absolutely not hearing your neighbor (until you want to) is essential.

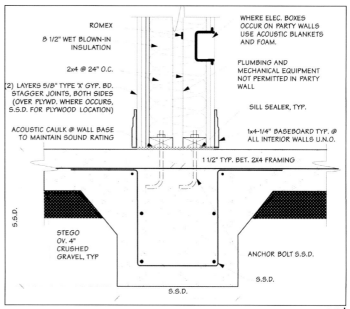

of $125 per square foot. This figure was essential to the architects' design and for material selection. This workshop also brought closure to and synthesized all of the previously created pieces. Durrett presented the final schematic design to QV, although the location of the buildings on the site could be adjusted as needed. Building plans, elevations, and general design details were also presented for approval. Once the group came to a consensus, the plans were ready to go to the city for approval.

QV's story was told in about fifty drawings that illustrated the proposed neighborhood. The Design Closure Workshop married the changes QV made to the house plans, the adjustments they made to the site plan, and hundreds of other adaptations. Ostensibly these drawings had to be thorough enough to convince the city that this was a project it could support. Durrett knew, however, that if he could make the group happy, he could make the city happy too. The drawings (including relevant details) needed to tell QV's story and clearly reflect who they wanted to be. So among other things, the drawings made it clear that the project was appropriate and fitting, and that it could and would fit the stated budget. Thank goodness the group had been so hands on during the design process. They could answer all of the questions and be much more convincing than a regular developer. No developer could have answered, for example, why the parking was so far from the houses (and hundreds

Chuck walked the group through the entire design for seven hours. Throughout it he asked, "What would you like changed before we go to the city?" Residents made commentary throughout the day. In the photo above, a resident makes a comment about the final design.

In the end, almost nothing was changed by city officials, which is a testament to how thoroughly the group's questions, challenges, concerns, hopes, and dreams had been addressed over the previous months.

of other important questions where the group was breaking the mold). People often ask Durrett, what is the secret ingredient to good cohousing design— "Lots of fully facilitated participatory meetings where this group can truly reach their potential as a community and a high function village."

On May 18, 2015, once the site plan, common house plan, and residential floor plans were complete, they submitted their application to the city for designation as a planned unit development (PUD). The approval process included several negotiated changes, which included assuring the fire marshal that a fire truck could get in and out. A public hearing took place in December 2015. At this hearing, the future neighbors of QV weighed in. Their input was mostly positive, though there were a few objections. The neighbors told the hearing officer "how wonderful" the project was, but "just don't build it on that piece of land." QV had worked hard to get the support of neighbors, and ultimately a few objections were not

Carts keep the fire lane car-free and people-rich.

Making a Car-Free Village

Cohousing groups have an excellent track record getting approval from cities because the residents "own" all of the design decisions and can explain and defend them. QV preserved open space by pooling their parking, keeping it remote, and keeping the site car-free. Remote parking in a senior-oriented neighborhood or facility is unheard of in America. Interestingly, a neighbor even complained about this at the public hearing, stating, "Isn't it a shame you're making those old people walk so far?" Port Townsend would never have allowed this unless dozens of residents had been prepared to describe the benefits of this plan and to make a case for it. They had to do so in order to overcome pushback from the neighbors and to avoid the classic city planner's excuse, "That's how we always do it." The residents of QV successfully made their case, and their remote parking plan was approved. Residents get to stroll through their neighborhood where they see folks working in their yards, doing laundry, and prepping for common meals, and someone might want to give them an update on the local news. Instead of three or four trips from the garage to the kitchen with groceries, they only have one trip (featuring a news update) while all the items roll along in a cute wagon.

enough to derail the project. The final approval of the PUD was issued on December 11, 2015—seven months from submission.

QV experienced a relatively speedy PUD approval process. Some projects take significantly longer to approve.

Design Workshop 5: Design Development

In Design Workshop 5, QV worked toward finalizing decisions having to do with material products.

If it's going to be economical, it has to look simple. It can be elegant but has to be eminently buildable.

Durrett presented his choices for the top 100 most important materials, going through each one at a time: siding, roofing, windows, flooring options, and so on. This intense review process went on for an entire day, and it included discussion of the suggested larger products, such as the engineering, structural, and mechanical systems. Also discussed were details about the proposed heating system (why it was recommended and how much it would cost to run), the thermostats, the radiators, and the light fixtures. No detail was too large or small. For example, they discussed how the preferred bathroom sink and faucet fit into the budget, and why one particular shower mixing valve was preferred over another (the preferred one helped quiet the flow of water so that one neighbor couldn't hear the other taking a shower).

QV's Design Team had one month to consider the list. Members were asked to send the chair of the Design Team a "love letter" that described any products they didn't like and why. He started getting letters later that afternoon. Again, no detail was too small. "We need to reconsider the kitchen sink," someone said, "and the faucet too." Two or three dozen products were reconsidered as a result of this process, but when the value of these products, the cost, the maintenance, the durability, and so on were considered, most of the original materials were kept. Only five were replaced with new and improved products.

Once QV had completed this material products review, the architects produced the construction documents: detailed plans and specs. Now QV could begin the contractor selection process, submit a preliminary loan application, and apply for building permits.

Design Workshop 6: Design Prioritization

Before QV could begin construction, they had to complete the Design Prioritization workshop. In this workshop, the group predecides what would be cut if the contractor's bid was too high. In order to do this, amenities were prioritized for the private houses and the common house. In this way they determined what would be standard in each home and in the common house, and what might be optional.

Items were reviewed and prioritized with the resident group. From there, they created a final prioritization list. Items they wanted that didn't make the cut were metal roofs, an exercise room, and a community hot tub. Items that stayed were a workshop, enhanced sound buffering, an art studio, a bike barn, and a storage facility. They also made enhancing energy efficiency a priority.

Design Workshop 7: Physical Plant Maintenance Program (PPMP)

This last design workshop is a bit different than the others because it doesn't focus on Design. Instead, it is a method by which the architect tries to ensure that the community fully understands what care their new homes require. This all-day workshop was done after the project was complete and the residents had moved-in. It was timed this way so that there would be fewer distractions, and so the residents could fully appreciate what they were being told. During Workshop 7, QV learned how to successfully

Scandinavian style.

Warm & cozy

QV hosting a group of tourists.

maintain their houses, the site, and the common facilities. This workshop included a site walk with all residents, guided by Durrett. The project manager, contractors, and job supervisor also joined.

Durrett began the walk outside. He started by saying, "Everything that you see here is of the earth and all of it is in a hurry to get back to the earth. It's called entropy. It's up to you to keep it up and well-maintained and to resist entropy." Together, as part of the all-day agenda, the residents went over the site drainage, preserving the wood trim, unclogging the house drain, cleaning out filters, turning off an errant smoke detector, and countless line items. At the end of the day, QV's Maintenance Team was well versed in the property's needs and was prepared to do their job.

QV took video of the walk-through, and they also designated their four-person Maintenance Team to pay the closest attention. That said, everyone participated so nothing was overlooked. Doing it as a group is important, and all the information needs to be shared with the entire community so that everyone can be proactively vigilant about their homes, the common facilities, and the site itself. As a result, they all can recognize when something needs attention.

1 + 1 = 3

Hundreds of design decisions are made every day during these workshops. If a group can brainstorm, discuss, and decide together, that means they will probably flourish as a cohousing community. People who effectively work together as a group quickly figure out cooperative math: 1+1=3. This translates into, "I have an idea, you have an idea, and together we can come up with a third idea that is better than either of our own ideas." This sort of cooperation is how an effective process is truly forged. Not everyone is capable of cooperating like this, and those folks quickly realize they are not cut out for cohousing, and so they go on their way.

A Thought on the Cohousing Process from Chuck Durrett

Creating cohousing requires many different participants engaged in many practical matters. For example, QV's local architect, Terrepin Architecture, helped the group finish the construction documents, McCamant and Durrett Architects completed the specifications, and we all shared the construction administration.

But building a neighborhood requires more than just completing tasks and checking off boxes. A new cohousing community is like a group of explorers who are crossing the Isthmus of Panama together. They are breaking new territory, finding a trail in the jungle, chopping a path with machetes, and watching their feet so as not to step into quicksand or on a deadly snake. The nights are spent in fitful worrying about spiders and other unknowns. If you have ever walked off a trail and into a real jungle, it only takes about a dozen feet for you to realize that this place is dark and scary, and that you are lost. But if you have a trail available to you, and a guide who has been down that trail many times before, then you would be wise to take it.

This is my request: Do not to try to cut corners while you're in the process of creating cohousing. What's more, do not let an errant alpha talk your group into doing things their way. You might save some money, but you will ultimately pay more in terms of both time and money. It's also possible that the community you create won't be worth the effort to build, much less maintain.

There is a growing cohort of folks who have forged the trail. Seek them out. They will listen to your group, and they will design your cohousing community to fit your specific needs. You don't need to cut your own path through the jungle. This is the most important advice I can impart. The QV group hired experienced cohousing professionals (including Katie McCamant and I—not only for the initial workshops but also the many evenings I spent with them after the workshops talking about key and timely issues). And it paid off.

QV traveled through the jungle together and arrived safely and securely at their final destination.

Architect tour with resident initiator, Pat Hundhausen, as her kitchen cabinets were being installed in her new home. It's times like this that I wish I owned a selfie stick.

10

"Good buildings come from good people, and all problems are solved by good design."
— *Stephen Gardiner*

Constructing Quimper Village

CONSTRUCTING ANY NEW PROJECT is a challenge, and a cohousing development presents its own unique challenges and special considerations. And the number one special consideration is the level of care required to avoid cost increases.

Once the schematic drawings are done and approved, the construction documents are drawn up, the building permits finalized, and bank financing is complete, it's time to start construction.

A key issue during the construction phase is the budget. QV closely monitored the work itself, as well as the budget. They were mindful that a handful of households could get squeezed out if the project experienced budgetary overruns. This required the new community to exercise discipline and resist the temptation to add extras beyond what they had worked so hard to agree upon during their workshops.

Recall that QV had established three basic home types, and that they worked hard to find agreement on things like fixtures, flooring, and countertops. They did this because building costs are kept down when materials are purchased in bulk and homes are built to standard specifications.

QV worked closely with their builder, Fairbank Construction Company, and their architects to ensure the work was done right the first time, on time and on budget. The result was a meaningful collaboration and a great success. There's a long, long list of what can be successfully prevented if someone who knows what they are looking for can put a finger in the dam before things get out of hand. The reality is that the economic downturn of 2008 changed everything. Far too few artisans survived, so vigilant architects have to play a much bigger role than before. In the case of QV,

Stick by stick, the western world goes together.

the right builder played a big role in their success.

There's a long list of construction considerations that, when under considered, add up to too much money. It can get unsustainable quickly. After more than fifty projects, McCamant and Durrett Architects has a keen eye for identifying unnecessary cost increases. Quality compromises, or long-term maintenance liabilities, mean that cohousing groups historically have been able to avoid the lack of structural strapping that leads to considerable issues down the line.

The first spade by Pat Hundhausen.

Bring in the fill dirt!

The CIT

The CIT Team, from left to right, Mena Quilici, Jerry Spieckerman, Carolyn Salmon, Bill Darlington.

In every project, there needs to be a small team of residents that keeps apprised of construction issues and communicates them to the group. We refer to this group as a Construction Interface Team (CIT). The group discusses delays and other issues that may impact site visits. They are also available to answer questions about how the project is progressing. This is how the CIT saw and implemented their role at QV.

The **Construction Interface Team** is a group of four or five residents who take it upon themselves to:
- Interface between the property owner and the contractor
- Interface with the group and design architect
- Interface with the group and local architect
- Interface with the group and project manager
- Interface with the group and neighbors
- Develop site access policies, including:
    a. Signed releases
    b. Insurance requirements
    c. Schedule whole group visits
- Develop a Maintenance Committee
    a. Roles and responsibilities
    b. Financial obligations
- Develop a punch list
    a. Roles and responsibilities
    b. Member involvement and process for individual homes
- Oversee homeowner orientations
    a. Develop a process
    b. Define roles and responsibilities
    c. Manage documentation of home systems and appliances

A collection of photos from the early phases of construction. The builders continued through the rain, winter weather and wind. It was impressive. And you could see the great pride in actually making something, and the great appreciation of the future residents who visited each month. Chuck's agreement with the residents was that he would not forward his field notes and corrections to them as long as the fixes were made. And Fairbank always made the fixes.

An Interview with David Wrinkle
Project Manager, Fairbank Construction.

Chuck: Some contractors that get involved with cohousing are too focused as a company on custom work, and some too exclusively, like home builders, on production. Production can be characterized as organized and efficient, usually rapid but not always the highest craftsmanship. It can even be characterized as even forgiving. Custom is more methodical, to the point of a few folks standing around with their hands on their hips trying to figure out what they are going to do next. Obviously, production is less costly.

Fairbank appears to be able to strike a balance between the two. Mostly production but able to do custom when the special situation calls for it.

David: Fairbank worked out well because our company spans many different types of projects, from entry level homes to multi-million-dollar homes and developments. This variety enables us to perform production and craftsmanship at multiple levels.

We are a fairly large construction company in our area, which gives us a larger and more diversified manpower and subcontractor resource. This allows us to accommodate the requirements of different types of projects. Well-packaged projects prior to the selection of the general contractor are more likely to be efficient and productive at whatever level the project is designed to be. We believe that experienced managers who value relationships and communication are key to the success of any project.

We draw a tremendous amount of construction knowledge from two other divisions within our company and it makes sense. Fairbank Special Services provides our community with small repairs to home additions. Our commercial division has also been established for many years and has exposed us to a different perspective of construction technique than residential construction. But many of the basics are similar. Here we learn the discipline of budget and schedule contracts.

Chuck: To what extent do you believe that knowing these people in the context of a custom-made neighborhood made it easier to do that work. Was building a village more gratifying than just building real estate?

David: It is not easier to do warranty work for a group. If one thing goes wrong in one unit, everyone has to be notified to determine if they have the same issue. Then I plan to go to the village and do the warranty repairs…then we find out that not everyone responded and I have to spend time walking through all of the steps again to fix the same issue for others. This isn't always how it is, sometimes better, sometimes worse.

Now your comment about how gratifying it is as a village versus more traditional real estate. Well, I have had dinner with residents in the common house and I have always felt extremely appreciated. I think it would be better to answer something like, "How do you perceive to get the best value for what you are trying to achieve?" Answering that question provides a more holistic world where people know who they are building for.

Chuck: What can architects learn from working with an experienced contractor?

David: First and foremost, most architects seem to have very little experience with cost, and in particular, cost control. That was not the case with MDA architects. Because MDA have so much experience with fixed numbers, and because you know and care about cohousing so much, you therefore go the extra length to make sure that it works financially. But most of the time that is a big wrestling match, and everyone loses.

Chuck: What is special about working with a cohousing group? How did you help set them up for success, and how can they best help set you, Fairbank Construction, up for success? In regard to the cohousing aspect, what would you have done differently?

David: Stay way ahead on thinking through the work ahead (two to three months) in case I need group feedback. It made us better contractors as well. We noticed design and construction concerns as early as possible in order to set the group up for success. Work with an experienced architect, because they helped us stay ahead of pending issues.

On the following pages, we'll be showing some common erros that happened along the way. They prove that nothing shoulod be taken for granted, and to note that experience helps. And to note that while not uncommmon, these all have to be caught along the way. Antoher thing that makes cohousing exceptional is that it really is productive construction with custom expectations. That combination pushes the quality control vigilance in some areas.

What follows are a few photos to demonstrate this fact and to entertain.

Concrete stem wall is missing here. See detailed drawing on left.

The concrete foundation being constructed, but the concrete stem wall is missing.

The lumber has been put up for private houses.

These headers in interior, non-bearing walls are not necessary and cost too much.

The window sills need to be high enough to fit above the counter tops, as shown in the plans.

Strapping needed for custom column cap. The red shows three locations for strapping.

Straps over the beam may be needed. Consulting with a structural engineer is needed regarding stitching beams together.

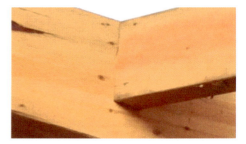

This top plate needs to be fitted with a 24-inch LST strap. Please lap all future top plates.

We recommend nailing with 21-24 16d nails.

Each 6 x 12 board needs to be supported all the way to the ground.

A crane is used while installing roof trusses.

A good way to do blown-in fiberglass insulation is with a mesh screen.

An Interview with Richard Berg
Terrapin Architects

Chuck: Richard, what was the biggest advantage of having a local architect on the project?

Richard: Well, first, I want to say that I'm looking forward to learning the whole process so that I can facilitate the next one in Port Townsend. Secondly, ostensibly we can help with the local city approval, but Chuck knows what he is looking for, and can help guide the locals. But someone has to go down to city hall.

Chuck: Then what?

Richard: During construction, the local architect is able to meet more often with the contractor, at lowest cost. A consistent on-site contact between the architect, contractor, and owner always increases the likelihood of project success.

The local architect may also have a better sense of when to consult McCamant and Durrett about construction questions than the contractor would have on their own. Reducing the number of construction site visits from McCamant and Durrett reduces the costs of travel and accommodations to the project.

Chuck: Then what?

Richard: The local architect can visit the site on short notice to troubleshoot and resolve issues. Immediate response to construction questions can keep the project moving and help avoid delays. The local architect can also take some pressure off McCamant and Durrett Architects. They can ask the local architect for help if they are pressed for time, and also less travel makes life easier and less stressful.

Chuck: What are your bulleted take away points?

Richard:
- We learned a lot about how to do cohousing.
- We enjoyed our working partnership with McCamant and Durrett Architects.
- We think the division of work turned out well.

- We enjoyed developing good working relationships during construction with both the Quimper village folks and the contractor.
- We learned that design discipline is important.
- We enjoyed being part of a successful team.

<u>Takeaways:</u>

We here at MDA Architects are motivated to prepare more and more local architects to do cohousing. But we also believe that to do it right takes more effort than is obvious. After studying cohousing architecture for a year in Denmark, Kate and I went back after our degree for what was intended to be full-time-6-months of figuring out what process works best for designing and building cohousing. However, it was clear at that point that we didn't know what we were doing yet. These buildings house high functioning social structures clad in better than average architecture. I believe that it would be nothing less than unethical to take a penny from anyone until we were fully trained – just like you don't fly a passenger plane until you are certified. And the best practitioners in the world convinced us to stay to get adequately trained. So, we did. We designed another senior cohousing community in which the group had hired three other architects before they hired us. It cost them three years and $100K. Richard came to four of our eight standard workshops with the group (Getting-It-Built Workshop, Construction Material Workshop, Design Prioritization Workshop, and Physical Plant Maintenance Program Workshop). I suggested that he come to the other four soon and do the next cohousing project in Port Townsend. There is one on the horizon.

Whatever a day or two delay costs, it pales in comparison to going back to a finished house to add a post in a wall that's already gyp boarded. Scheduling too often drives a project, not quality construction.

This header space is ready for insulation as detailed (bottom right).

It's important to insulate above headers. We recommend a pour-in asbestos-free vermiculite product such as Schundler Vermiculite extra fine Block and Cavity Fill or a slow-rise foam such as FoamPower Handi-Flow. (pour in through a half-inch diameter hole)

Insulate boxed corners. We recommended drilling holes in sheathing and insulating from the exterior.

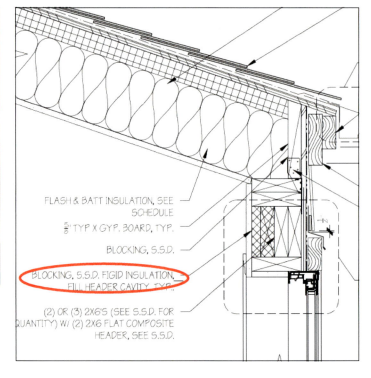

Detailed drawing for rigid insulation detail at header.

VERY IMPORTANT! Strap top of not-lapped top plates.

Absolutely must have LST strap connecting beam to top plate.

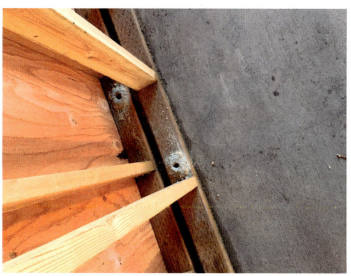

Missing anchor bolts. Do not cover up!

Specified as 2x4 staggered stud on 2x6 plate with sound insulation at living to bedroom wall.

Acousto-plumb, a sound-mitigating product, is required at copper pipes at party wall.

No Lowry pad at this party wall, and hole is overcut. Needs Lowry pad and foam.

Please, no hot and cold water lines touching!

Lowry pads at back of outlets on party wall. This is important for acoustics and fire safety.

Pour-on-site concrete fire lane is started after most of the building constructions are done.

2x6 cedar trim at top of frame out (not 2x8 at bottom).

Future residents touring their "promised" home.

Assure area drains (just out of front door) are low enough. Should be 12 inches below the floor height.

An Interview with Fred Kimball
Project Manager, Quimper Village

Chuck: What was unique about being the project manager for a cohousing effort?

Fred: Other than the entire concept of the project being unique, probably working with the construction committee was something I had never had to do before. Being the owners' representative (project manager) is different that being the PM for the contractor, there is a different finesse to getting something done without breaking the chain of command. Fortunately, we had a great contractor and I meshed well with their management team.

Chuck: I often argue that the project manager's real job is to ask yourself what problems to solve today? Is that true?

Fred: It certainly is one of the important tasks. I try to look into what's happening tomorrow or the next day and think about the tripping points that the trade people might hit and get to them before they go down the wrong path. By approaching them in casual conversation about upcoming tasks you can get a sense of whether or not they understand where they are heading. I would also quiz the site superintendent about what tasks were going on, who he thought the weakest link was, and I would try to keep an eye on the crew.

Chuck: I often argue that the hardest problem for a project manager is to recognize the 20% of the project management problems that they don't know how to solve, and then to figure out who to hire to get that job done. Is that true?

Fred: I don't know if I could quantify it but it is true that you need to recognize issues well before hand and brainstorm solutions with the management team (site superintendent, contractor PM, architects, and engineers, etc.). This is especially true if there are details that are difficult to do and there are other ways to accomplish them. For example, if there are local techniques that would be easier for the construction team to use because that's the way they're used to doing things. I'm fond of saying it's not the path but the destination, but you

Fred Kimball (right) leads a group of residents touring the constructing site.

have to be careful in the trades, don't stray too far and become inefficient with either time or materials.

Chuck: Let's talk big picture. You have been an important member of the larger Port Townsend community (population 9,000) for a long time, and you have played a big role in housing solutions in this town– Habitat for Humanity and more. What role does this new project, the one and only senior cohousing project in Port Townsend, play in the well-being of local seniors and the health of town altogether.

Fred: I think it's a great addition to our community. When I am asked about Quimper Village, I tell people that the members hit a home run with the project! What I was most impressed with is how well they were functioning as a group before construction even started and how they were able to "hit the ground running" upon move in. For the members living in the community and participating, it can only be beneficial to them. I'd say that this was the true magic that you, Chuck, pulled off with all the training exercises they went through before and during construction. Too many of these types of planned communities stumble and stagger through the early days of being thrown together as a group and never really reach full potential. I hope as our community moves forward addressing our housing crisis that cohousing is included in the discussion for solutions and that the Quimper folks join in the conversation. I have built primarily for retired folks and as they begin to age past being freshly retired I think many of them would fit into this model. While it may not fit all, I find it hard to believe that many would not enjoy the lifestyle once experienced. I think it's important for society to learn to live smaller and part of that is to live more local hence be more community driven.

Do these photos represent what a modern-day village looks like? For now, yes!. We fully expect them to get more and more economical and easier to build.

113

11

"Home is where your story begins..."
— Annie Danielson

Living There: Was It All Worth It?

WHAT'S LIFE LIKE THERE NOW?

When we started this design project in 2015, the average age for the group was seventy-two and a half years old. They say again and again that they wished they had started earlier–when they were younger.

Every time I hear that, I think about a senior cohousing community in Roskilde, Denmark, where all of the five couples that started the project were in their early fifties. They were proactive. And what was so unique was their mission statement. It simply read, "We're going to have as much fun our second fifty years as we did our first fifty years." And I'm pretty sure that if they have fun along the way, they will live lighter on the planet in the process and accomplish that mission statement by listening to and loving each other. They will honor each other much more, and honor their time together, and because they like being together, they will, in the cohousing fashion, solve the problems of the day. That's what cohousers do when they get together. Cohousing problems are city-wide problems. That's why Bill McKibben wrote in Chuck's book *Creating Cohousing* that what he appreciated about cohousing most was not how much energy they save compared to their former residencies, but how much positive energy they create, wherever they are.

In the case of QV, if they had started earlier, they could have enjoyed the community they created for much longer.

Do all of these good folks know

Dancing happens.

each other, care about each other, and support each other as much as they thought they might? Well, go back and read the interviews again, or go to Port Townsend and check it out for yourself. Or you can just look at the photos and draw your own conclusions. In any case, I have to say after visiting well over 300 cohousing communities around the world, this one garners as many smiles per half hour (an important metric) as any other livable, lovable community I have visited.

I had planned to go to Denmark in February 2019 to see a new, and widely considered state-of-the-art, senior cohousing community there. But I decided to go to Port Townsend instead and interview people who, from what I could discern, had set the new bar for state-of-the-art in the United States.

Quimper Village Residents' Own Words

We have settled into a rhythm and routine that matches our expectations for our supportive community and we're busy living and thriving in our new homes. We've got things to do on the calendar: common dinners (of course), movie nights, chair yoga, tai chi, rustic croquet, monthly birthday parties of Trivial Pursuit games with chocolate prizes, game nights, and concerts. And of course, we have our beloved jigsaw puzzle freaks. We can join the group on Friday mornings to discuss the more personal events in our lives in an arena that is designed to be encouraging and supportive.

We are artists of all abilities and have filled our common house with our successful products. You should have seen our neighbors dressed as a set of matching salt and pepper shakers for Halloween! There's no such thing as a holiday orphan around here.

We have a camaraderie of living

Art shows happen.

Art class happens.

Courtyard parties happen.

Real life happens and people need each other. Those relationships are stitched together over time.

together and are facing the surprises that time presents. This is a place where you can call a neighbor at 4:00 a.m., ask for a ride to the hospital, and be on the road in fifteen minutes. We've had a rash of joint replacements, but all is well now because we live in a physical setting that is without steps and we are surrounded by neighbors who care. We've also shared the grief of a few deaths. To honor those who have left us, we developed an onsite memorial grove.

Was it worth doing? Absolutely, YES! You will get the most out of senior cohousing by joining in your fifties and sixties. I have an eighty-two-year-old friend who says he's not ready for this yet, and unfortunately, he's missed out on years of neighborly companionship. This is not where you go to end your life; it's where you go to live. Physically, it's a lot easier to downsize and move when you're younger instead of waiting for a medical crisis and realizing you're left with unappealing options.

We've learned that we're a little light on young, strong muscles, and that we need to hire out some of the heavy work to respect and care for each other. Time together brings opportunities for personal growth and knowledge, which leads us to inventive new solutions that come along the way with the joys of life.

May we all thrive in our years ahead!

Appendix A
WHAT WE DID RIGHT?
Written by QV Group

1. Discovered and read *Senior Cohousing Handbook, 2nd Edition*, by Charles Durrett.
2. Did a presentation at the Unitarian Fellowship on senior cohousing as an option for aging followed by the ten week **STUDY GROUP 1** course with 20 participants (facilitated by a future Quimper Village Member).
3. Scheduled and marketed the **Getting-It-Built Workshop** at the end of Study Group 1, hired Charles Durrett to do six workshops and design Quimper Village, and hired Katie McCamant to be our Development Consultant.
4. Identified **LAND SITES** in our town that might be appropriate for a senior cohousing community (Site Team). Optioned two properties with the help of Charles Durrett and contracted to buy one soon after the **Getting-It-Built Workshop**.
5. Hired a process consultant and learned **DYNAMIC GOVERNANCE, A CONSENT MODEL**, to facilitate our meetings and set up our organization (Process Team).
6. Hired a highly experienced **LOCAL PROJECT MANAGER** on an hourly basis to oversee our project. Tasks included navigating our project through the city bureaucracy.
7. Created **TEAMS OF AUTHORITY** to get work done in specific areas; i.e., Membership, Marketing, Process, Legal and Financial, Social, E-communications, Landscape, etc.
8. Offered informative **SENIOR COHOUSING PRESENTATIONS** at different venues in our region including a weekend in Port Townsend where we scheduled a cohousing presentation, a tour of the town, a potluck, and provided a list of other things to do (Marketing and ad hoc Teams).

9. Hired an **ATTORNEY** to legally organize Quimper Village; first into an LLC, then, upon review of Washington state law, into a Washington State Cooperative, which provided us with legal protection because we were asking people to put money at risk (Finance and Legal Team).
10. Adopted a **REGULAR BY-MONTHLY ALL–MEMBER MEETING** schedule always open to visitors (Process Team).
11. Set up **A WEB PAGE AND FACEBOOK PAGE** that is continually updated and created a monthly newsletter eventually sent to five hundred contacts (E-Communication Team).
12. Marketed **"QUIMPER VILLAGE, BE PART OF THE DREAM"** at different times with flyers at the farmer's market and around town, newspaper articles, opinion pieces and ads, local radio interviews, a Quimper Village car in a local parade, business cards, brochures, bumper stickers, logo pins, and word of mouth (Marketing Team).
13. Held monthly **COFFEE AND CONVERSATION** groups in private homes for people interested in joining Quimper Village where we described our process to date and answered questions (Marketing Team).
14. Prepared **VISITOR, ASSOCIATE, AND MEMBER PACKETS** that contained our history and described our Associate and Membership fees and requirements (Membership Team).
15. PRESCREENED prospective Associate Members with a "Personal Profile" and a financial disclosure form we asked them to fill out. We also required that they be pre-approved for a mortgage even if they could pay cash (Membership and Finance and Legal Team).
16. Held frequent **SOCIAL GATHERINGS** after meetings for holidays and special anniversaries. Held picnics on the property, small group dinners, and small group game nights in individual homes (Social Team).
17. Hired a Process Consultant to teach **NON-VIOLENT COMMUNICATION** skills over a several week period. This led to the development of a monthly Friday Forum where Associates and Members could come together to talk about non business issues, navigate differences, laugh, and enjoy each other in a relaxed, somewhat structured setting (Process Team).
18. Developed a financial plan requiring Households to put in Required Capital Contributions (RCC's) on a schedule until Quimper Village could provide 22% of the capital needed for the cost of the project ($10.4 million total). This provided us with the collateral we needed for our bank loan as well as providing each Household with the down payment on their home.

19. Elected five **CONSTRUCTION INTERFACE TEAM** (CIT) Members to be liaisons between our professionals and Members while we were under construction (all Members).
20. Vetted eight **CONSTRUCTION COMPANIES** and interviewed three to select the most appropriate company to build Quimper Village with the assistance of our local Project Manager, Development Consultant (Katie McCamant), and architects.
21. Submitted information packets about our proposed project to two banks and **SELECTED ONE BANK** for our construction loan.

LESSONS WE LEARNED

1. Let the group decisions stand that were made in the original workshops; e.g., exterior paint colors. If a decision is revisited, it usually creates "churn" among the group and the new decision almost always does not work as well as the original decision.
2. Organize **initial legal structure to protect ourselves as we were putting other people's money at risk** (We organized as an LLC initially and then needed to reorganize into a Washington State Cooperative based on the counsel of our lawyer).
3. Limit the amount of time for Associate Members to remain in the group; e.g., three months. (Some of our Associate Members highly influenced several decisions that were made and then were withdrawn).
4. Emphasize over and over again that "production construction" trumps custom homes. (Custom features drive up costs for everyone).

Appendix B
Quimper Village Guidelines for Team Decisions
Sociocracy used to manage, but not design Quimper Village

Managing the day-to-day functions of Quimper Village, including maintaining our facilities and grounds, prioritizing work, controlling our budgets, **enhancing our community**, and making decisions as to how we use and manage our common space is the primary responsibility of the Quimper Village Functional Teams. Teams have responsibilities and authorities covering all of the major areas of community management such that very few decisions need to be made by the community as a whole.

Teams are, however, encouraged to bring issues to the whole community if they think a decision will be controversial or if a better decision would result, even though the team may have the authority to make the decision on their own. A team decision that is expected to have a **permanent or significant** impact on the land and community may warrant input before the decision is made. **Examples might be:**

- **Building a structure**
- **Making a change that requires all or most members to do something**
- **Making a change that creates an expense or legal commitment**
- **Making a decision that other team members would have a reasonable expectation of knowing and being involved in.**

Team Assumptions and Responsibilities
- All decisions will be made with the intention of having the best interests of the community in mind and will be well thought out and researched prior to implementation.
- The membership at large will be informed about any decisions that are made outside of the larger group process through minutes, announcements, or reports.

- If there is any "fuzziness" regarding what level the decision needs to be made at, then it will pass up a level (Subteam > Functional Team Authority > Coordinating Team > Membership).
- A team can choose to bring a decision to the entire membership if they believe there is value in including everyone in the discussion, even though an individual or team has authority to make the decision.
- If any member has concerns about how decisions are being made, they will bring their concerns forward to the team to allow for an open and honest discussion of the issues.

Team Authority

Teams are responsible for assessing the level of participation required for any decision, and for determining whether a decision is important enough to be made by the group as a whole, or whether it can be made within the teams.

Function Teams Have Authority

In addition to the specific responsibilities and authorities for each team, all Functional Teams have responsibility and full authority for the following:

- Establishing the aims and goals of their team **within the requirements in the Declaration and area of responsibility of the Team.**
- Electing team leaders **(leaders not included for the Functional Teams, delegates, facilitators, and secretaries).**
- Decisions related to ongoing team management.
- Maintaining team meeting minutes.
- **Managing the team's budget within the requirements established by the Treasurer and the Finance & Legal Team.**
- **Proper handling of funds received by the team, if any, in accordance with the requirements established by the Treasurer and the Finance & Legal Team.**
- Communicating to the membership all significant team issues under consideration, decisions, and events (including distributing agendas prior to meetings).
- Maintaining a chores list of work needed to manage and maintain the areas of responsibility within their team and working with the Chores Team to ensure that the work gets done.

Criteria for Assessing Team Decision Authority

Teams must consider that while they have much autonomy in making decisions within the scope of their teams, they also have responsibility to bring some decisions up to the Coordinating Team or Membership.

Teams should consider the following questions to assess whether a decision can be made within a team or whether it needs a broader discussion and decision. If there are any "no" answers to the following questions, the team must readdress the decision to ensure all issues have been addressed or take the decision to the next team level.

1. Does the decision conform to existing **Community Agreements, Articles of Incorporation, By-laws, and Declaration**?
2. Is the decision within **the area of responsibility of the team**?
3. Is the decision consistent with the current uses of the Common Space?
4. Are there sufficient member resources to accomplish the task being considered?
5. Is there a potential for future impacts to affect the shared facilities, land or budget?
6. Has the community been informed of the topic or action with the adequate time for a broader participation in a decision?

If a team determines that an item should go to either the Coordinating Team or full membership, the team can request assistance from the Process Team to help them structure a discussion or proposal for full consensus. **Teams can also request assistance from the Finance & Legal Team in reviewing the proposal against the governing documents of the Village before presenting it.**

Appendix C
Inspirational Talk for General Meeting
May 5, 2016

By **Pat Hundhausen**

    As I am sure you all know, two Quimper Village households withdrew from our community last week. I am, as I imagine many of you are, feeling a range of emotions from anger to sadness to being a little scared. It is a challenging time on our community-building journey—we can't quite remember the vision of our beginning and cannot quite see the end when we all move in and live happily ever after. We are in the middle, and middles are often hard. Our budget came in 20% over our estimation. Despite our CIT clarifying and calming us with a comprehensive presentation regarding their value engineering efforts, many of us became distressed and anxious when our California architect went over the same ground, only differently, at a recent meeting with him. Today, we find ourselves living in ambiguity about the cost of our houses and with two C units to sell several weeks before we hope to break ground. So, we each ask ourselves the question again, "Will living in this community really work?"

    In countless ways, it has worked! Using professionals when we needed them, we have researched available properties and bought land, designed a site plan, a Common House, and three different-sized living units. We have organized legally twice, written by-laws and community agreements, navigated through the City's rules and regulations to a Public Hearing last December where the Hearing Officer rated our project a ten out of ten! We have set up a Membership plan which has been repeatedly revised to meet our changing needs. We have designed a landscaping plan for our site, implemented and updated a marketing plan that has continuously recruited new members, implemented a governance model which supports equivalence, transparency, and efficiently run meetings. We have managed hundreds of thousands of dollars responsibly. We have vetted Construction Companies thoroughly and interviewed banks to secure a construction loan. Our CIT has spent countless hours reviewing construction drawings and requesting updates of our professionals. We have built the nonphysical part of our community through socials, small group activities, and picnics. We have created a Friday Forum to learn nonviolent communication, empathy, and conflict resolution. We have created an e-communication system to keep visitors, associates, and members continuously in the loop on what is happening everywhere in our community. We have done all this with huge amounts of hard work and very little acrimony. We've brought our skill sets to the table from lifetimes of work and experience and we have learned many new things. We have been busy and connected in ways many of us have not been before in our lives. We have set out to build one of a very few senior cohousing communities in the United States as well as the first senior cohousing community in the state of Washington.

We have had and we will continue to have bumps along the way. We have made and we will make more mistakes. That' a reality! But we have become proactive about our own aging. We have pioneered an option for those who come after us. And we've done this with our own grit, perseverance, and focus because we believe that there is a better way to grow older. And that is to live in a human community where we can remain in control and connected, where we can share our resources, live lighter on the planet, care for one another, and have fun together.

More than ever, we need to stay focused, moving forward one step at a time on our Critical Path! Working together, we have done this! Working together, we can do this! Working together, we will do this!

Appendix D

This is an **invitation** to the QV group to come to a final workshop with the architect and the contractors

"What you see is of the earth; and in a hurry to get back to the earth."

July 17, 2017

Dear Quimper Village Cohousers,

I would like to personally invite each and every one of you to the very important **Physical Plant Maintenance Program Workshop** on Thursday, Sept 28, 2017, from 9:00 am – 4:30 pm. We will meet in the Common House at 9:00 am. This is when you will learn how to successfully maintain your buildings (the physical plant) for many years to come.

Please think of this workshop as the conclusion to the design workshops: "It doesn't pay to design an organ if no one knows how to play it." Or in this case, it is an orchestra—dysfunctional if everyone is playing a different score. When it comes to the long-term social success, this workshop is just as important as every other. Deferred maintenance saddles subsequent years with less happiness. And the meetings that go along with deferred maintenance are never fun, "Now why didn't we deal with this two years ago?" As you know our office mantra is, "If it doesn't work socially, why bother?" If you don't take care of the buildings, the community will suffer.

Although most of you have successfully maintained your own houses for years, doing so in a cohousing community is different and requires additional skills and systems. The "tragedy of the commons," is real. "Oh, I thought that someone else was going to take care of this," or "Oh, I thought you were," or "I thought somebody would notice that." Or my favorite, "Oh I just assumed that that was being taken care of." In this way, deferred maintenance inadvertently happens all the time, because one individual didn't know what to do about it, or thought someone else was looking after it, or didn't even know that it was a problem in the first place.

This workshop will address tasks that need to be performed regularly as well as signs that a problem has occurred. The workshop will cover many items that are entirely your responsibility, for instance internal plumbing fixtures and the internal paint job.

In addition to maintaining the interior of your own home, each resident also has the responsibility to help the maintenance committee succeed. For instance, there are things that will occur in your own house that pertain to the whole building. Every individual needs to know what those things are so that they can report anomalies/problems to others if necessary, or better yet, so they can readily remedy them themselves. Think of doing it yourself as an act of independence and privacy: others won't need to tromp through your house to inspect things if you can report them yourself. You can just let the maintenance committee know about that little black spot, the size of a quarter, before it becomes a black spot the size of my black beret—possibly a leak in the exterior wall or an internal plumbing leak.

In past workshops, a few cohousers have asked, "Why does everyone have to come? I'm not going to be on the Maintenance Committee, and I don't know anything anyway." Maintenance may look hard or intimidating to some, but this workshop will make the information accessible. It's where you will learn how to turn the water off when your faucet breaks and lots and lots of other fun stuff, and it's important to know where and how to notice problems and therefore report them to others.

Think of this workshop just like the earlier workshops where the agenda is tried and true. Maintenance is too often the Achilles heel of cohousing because "someone else volunteered to take care of it," so therefore I have no responsibility. Wrong—your responsibility is to set those volunteers up for success. So, this workshop is the absolutely best way of solving these problems—with knowledge. When everyone does this workshop the knowledge becomes common, and it is much less of an issue later.

Everything in the project is of the earth, and everything is in a hurry to get back to the earth—that's entropy. You are now the stewards. I don't mean this to be condescending, but too many projects suffer from deferred maintenance. Maintenance can be a positive and community-building experience, even spiritual. Or it can be the source of wasted meetings and significant acrimony. We propose the former.

It is important that whoever plans to live in Quimper Village attend this workshop, if at all possible. The purpose of this workshop is:

(A) To create a comprehensive and common knowledge base as everyone hears the same thing and asks questions. The "dumber" the questions, the better for all, especially future residents who move in later. Long-term success is based on questions answered and you reminding the maintenance committee of issues in the future.

(B) To create a system so that knowledge is not lost over time. The workshop will be recorded on video to bring future new residents up to speed. They will then be the ones reminding early residents, "Hey on that video the roofer said that we should not do a roof repair on a hot day," etc., etc.

WORKSHOP SCHEDULE

9:00 am: Introduction by Chuck

9:30 am: Exterior envelope with Chuck and whomever FAIRBANK wants (gutters to dirt up against the footings)

10:00 am: Painting subcontractor + (FAIRBANK rep)

10:45 am: Electrical subcontractor + (FAIRBANK rep)

11:30 am: Plumbing subcontractor + (FAIRBANK rep)

12:30 pm: Lunch

1:15 pm: Heating/cooling subcontractor + (FAIRBANK rep)

2:00 pm: Cabinet subcontractor + (FAIRBANK rep)

2:30 pm: Flooring subcontractor + (FAIRBANK rep)

3:15 pm: Roofing subcontractor + (FAIRBANK rep)

3:45 pm: Landscape, irrigation subcontractor, and site drainage + (Chuck and FAIRBANK rep)

4:30 pm: Adjourn

The contractor, a representative from each subcontractor (and hopefully Richard and Fred), and I will walk us all through each of these meetings. I will start each session with key questions and issues. Fairbank will coordinate the installer participant (to have the person who installed that work there for that time, e.g. the plumber).

We will also need two videographers. (With much respect, we've had too many cases where too much footage was lost: "Oh, I have to go," or "Oh, my battery died," or they dropped the camera and it stopped working. But my favorite is, "I accidentally deleted the footage.") Without all of the footage being viewed by all new members, maintenance will be compromised. A video must be handed to each new household when they move in. New members are the best ally in maintenance because they are the person who has watched the video most recently and they catch all the things that the group has been taking for granted.

We have had the best long-term success when thirty-five future residents troop around with us. The residents share with other residents and help raise even better questions, and in turn it keeps maintenance issues to a minimum and accountability to a maximum.

This will also be our last formal get together. I just want everyone here to know that it has been a very meaningful experience working with you. I'm just sorry that my mentor, Danish architect, Jan Gudmand Hoyer didn't get a chance to see this place. He passed on March 6, but I'm certain that he would have said that American cohousing has arrived.

Thanks very much for the opportunity and I'm looking forward to seeing everyone there.

Thanks,

Charles R. Durrett
Principal Architect

Appendix E
Quimper Village Development's Timeline

Forum: Quimper Village? Let's Talk! (Pat & David Hundhausen) — **January 28, 2014**

Study Group One: Aging Successfully Workshops (PDH) (See chapter 7 in the *Senior Cohousing Handbook*) — **April-June 2014**

Organizing, membership developement, establishing governance and decision-making processes, marketing, educating ourselves (QV members) — **June 2014**

Look for Land (QVM) — **July 2014**

First vision statement approved: "We are a group of 20 families and individuals planning a co-housing development that addresses our needs for living and aging successfully in community while enriching our private lives. As we move along this path, we are endeavoring to maintain respect and consideration for one another, understanding that building community is a fluid, evolving process — **July 24, 2014**

to which each of us contributes. We look forward to the many discoveries and course corrections, and plan to do this with healthy consensus, growing grace, and plenty of good humor." (Talking points: "To have as much future. Second 50 years as we did the first.")

August 21, 2014	First member joins
September 2014	Dynamic Governance/Sociocracy adopted (except for the design process)
Sept 27-28, 2014	Getting-It-Built Workshop w/ Katie McCamant (Cohousing Solutions) & Chuck Durrett (McCamant and Durrett Architects). Group process, design process, city approval process, committees, legal ownership, budgets
October 2014	Retained attorney (Colette Kostelec) Established LLC (QV LLC) Optioned land for 6 months & started due diligence work Retained development consultant - Cohousing Solutions (CS) Identified design architect - Chuck Durrett (MDA) Schedule established: general meetings 1st and 3rd Thursdays/Saturdays, CT 2nd and 4th Thursdays. Every team reports every meeting
November 2014	Hired Project Manager (Fred) QV LLC officers approved
December 2014	Field trip to Bellingham cohousing
January 25, 2015	Four members attend Dynamic Governance workshop in Seattle

Course correction: Development of Offering Memorandums to meet WA securities requirements. Quimper Village LLC becomes Townsend Meadows Cooperative	**January-April 2015**
Site Development Workshop (MDA)	**Jan 31-Feb 3, 2015**
Common House Workshop (MDA)	**Feb 21-22, 2015**
Marketing: newspapers, Olympic music sponsor, movie theater, monthly Coffee and Conversation continue, magnetized door signs circulating, Rhody Parade event, fliers at farmers market, posters and fliers to nearby Quaker, UU, and Unity churches, AAUW. Business cards with website info	**Spring 2015** 
Private House Workshop (MDA)	**March 15-17, 2015**
Design Closure Workshop (MDA)	**April 2015**
Preliminary Planned Unit Development plan to city Create Development Budget & Cash Flow (CS) Develop Financing Plan—Required Capital Contributions (CS)	**May 18, 2015**
Purchased property seller carried loan with interest only 16 households committed to marketing at Rotary meeting	**June 2015**
Preliminary visits to various banks, shopping for construction loan (CS) CIT elected	**August 2015**

August 29, 2015	Materials Workshop (MDA)
August 30, 2015	Prioritization Workshop (MDA)
October 2015	Begin general contractor search Begin rotating dinners
November 2015	First class of Empathy in Action (Nonviolent Communication) which evolved into Friday Forums (Alex Bryan)
November 2015	Local architect hired to help MDA finish construction documents and help implement construction administration: Terrapin Architecture (TA)
Dec 14, 2015	Public hearing on PUD
December 2015	Construction specifications (MDA)
Jan 12, 2016	PUD approval from the city
Jan 26, 2016	Architectural and engineering plans to city (TA)
February 2016	Contractor interviews and final selection. Fairbank Construction hired (FC) Construction drawings completed (MDA, TA)
February 2016	Initial construction loan presentations to 22 member households
March 2016	Initial construction cost estimate (FC) Value engineering reduces construction costs (FC, MDA, QV LLC)

Construction drawings completed with changes (MDA, TA) Construction permit application to city (TA) Begin construction loan application	
Brainstorming: What must we do prior to move-in? Tasks, teams, agreements… Where's the Critical Path?	April, 2016
2 households withdraw and Pat does her "Inspirational Talk"	May 5, 2016
Ground-breaking ceremony!!! Monthly site visits start	July 2016
Construction loan approved (First Federal Bank) Every member signs loan for $7+ million Unit selection begins	August 2016
Construction loan closed through First Federal Bank (CS) Site work commenced (FC)	September 2016
Construction Administration (MDA, TA, Fred Kimmel)	Sept 2016-Sept 2017
Preliminary meeting with bank loan officers	January 2017
Last membership sold Language of QV bylaws changed from consensus to consent	February 2017
Last site visits: 7/29, 8/24, 9/30	Fall 2017

Sept 28, 2017	•	Occupancy Permits received Physical plant orientation (MDA)
Oct 21, 2017	•	First member moves in
Nov 1, 2017	•	Common house completed
Dec 1, 2017	•	One-year warranty period begins (FC) First common meal is prepared, Stone Soup

Common meal & ingredients for First Common Meal.

Senior Cohousing
Certification

Americans are fast and furious with the English language–especially when it comes to real estate. The business plaza without the *plaza*, the industrial park without the *park,* and there are many other examples. There are communities that inadvertently call themselves cohousing that are in fact very cohousing inspired, cohousing-like, and are lovely places for sure, but are not cohousing. I firmly believe cohousing needs to be certified for its continuing success, just as organic farming needed certification before it really took off in the U.S.

I get too many emails from folks saying how their cohousing community failed or never worked in the first place. This is invariably because some of the six criteria that are involved in cohousing were not employed. When cohousing is firing on all cylinders, there is not a more beautiful habitat to see–people know each other, care about each other, and support one another over time. Where cooperation is easy and natural and where the community is obvious, and you can measure it. This is especially true when it comes to senior cohousing.

This raises the question: What is cohousing (hence, validating its certification)?

The senior cohousing communities of **Oakcreek Cohousing** in Stillwater, Oklahoma; **Quimper Village** in Port Townsend, Washington; **Mountain View Cohousing** in Mountain View, California; **Wolf Creek Lodge** in Grass Valley, California; and **Silver Sage** in Boulder, Colorado, are great examples and models. Being clear what cohousing is, and by contrast what it isn't, preserves the integrity and credibility of cohousing over time. It is a form of consumer protection. The certification of a cohousing project, provided by Sage Senior Cohousing Advocates, is a critical aspect of this consumer protection for seniors. Certification ensures that cohousing continues to be a concept that people can rely on. Having an actual certification documentation can prove to be beneficial in helping city officials see that cohousing is not just a sound bite; it's a certain kind of neighborhood.

For example, in the fall of 2017, the city of Durham, North Carolina, asked the residents of **Village Hearth Senior Cohousing** to provide proof that they were in fact a cohousing community. That was critical because residents were asking for numerous favors, like less parking and less road (by about 1,000 feet, which would have cost a fortune) and numerous other things from the city in order to get the project done on budget, and in return the city wanted to see a certification. The city wanted to cooperate, but they also didn't want to be hoodwinked. The certification provided the reassurances that the city needed, and our requests were ultimately approved.

By contrast, a developer in Petaluma, California, called his project cohousing, even though it featured no resident participation and the design did nothing to promote community interaction. He told the city council it was cohousing, because he wanted to ride the coattails of a very successful but legitimate cohousing community in a neighboring town. The project was approved. The developer hoodwinked the city council and they were angry. How was the city council to know? They did not have a certification that said, "This is the genuine article." The upshot is that when real cohousing communities came to the table down the line, the head planner said, "Whatever you do, do not call it cohousing." They had been fooled once but would not be fooled twice. No other cohousing has been built in that town despite considerable interest.

Another example is in the city of Bellingham, Washington. Bellingham is home to a sweet, 33-unit cohousing community, a village really, that is reminiscent of a traditional settlement, where people know, care about, and support each other. The city council admired this project so much that they passed some code variances for the next developer who proposed a new cohousing project, allowing for a number of breaks. The developer took advantage of the breaks (less parking, more units) but did not build cohousing. The developer gamed the system, and gamed the city council, the proximate neighbors, and the consumers. As a result, building another new "cohousing" community in Bellingham will prove very difficult if not impossible. Interestingly, the two projects are right across the street from each other. One feels like a conventional suburb, except with too many houses and too few parking spaces and is devoid of life between the buildings. The other one feels like a village bustling with life.

To ensure that cohousing remains genuine and is not conflated with other housing models that are not as credible, please adhere to the following principles when creating your cohousing community or please do not call it cohousing.

Criteria That Define Cohousing:

1. Participation. Co-developed, co-designed, and co-organized with the future resident group. First and foremost, the future residents are an integral part of creating the future community.
2. A private home but also extensive common facilities that supplement and facilitate daily living. Common facilities are perceived as an extension of each resident's house and supplement each home. There must be practical reasons to bring people together. Common meals must be held at least once a week. There is no more timeless means of sustaining community than breaking bread together.
3. Designed to facilitate naturally oriented community interaction over time. Not auto oriented.
4. Almost entirely resident managed. The residents, who are the owners of their own homes, in a cohousing community have the privilege and responsibility of determining how they will organize themselves and the work (and play) of managing their own lives and homes.
5. No hierarchy in decision making. Cohousing is about cooperation rather than type of ownership. And, as it turns out, cooperation transcends ownership type.
6. No shared economy. Unlike that of the commune or sometimes a co-op structure, cohousing community members do not share personal income.

Being clear about nomenclature and certifying cohousing is about consumer protection. Selling "lake front" property without a lake is wrong. Selling housing without participation is not cohousing. Selling cohousing without the *co* (*co*-designed for example) means just selling real estate, without the value added by the *co*.

Unfortunately, the temptation to build senior housing without the co is based on the misconception that co-designing will slow the process down, but it actually speeds it up. When we co-developed/co-designed **Cotati Cohousing** in less than 3 years, Cotati outpaced the other three brand new projects surrounding it. Those three neighboring projects took 5, 5, and 7 years (respectively) to develop. They took longer to get through city approvals because they hadn't involved the future residents. For senior cohousing to continue to be faster to build and higher functioning than other senior housing alternatives, what is and isn't cohousing must be clearly defined and actively defended. Marketers are cavalier when it comes to real estate nomenclature, but our firm will continue to work hard to preserve the integrity of cohousing.

Our ultimate goal with this certification is consumer protection and ensuring that cohousing continues to be a concept that people can rely on. Having an actual document (this certification) proved to be beneficial in helping the city see that cohousing is not just hyperbolic marketing. In fact, it's a genuine.

Thanks to Pat Darlington, of **Oakcreek Cohousing**, and David and Pat Hundhausen, of Quimper Village Senior Cohousing, who co-authored this certification program. It is through individuals like these cohousers and the dedication of organizations like SAGE Cohousing International (sagecohousinginternational.org) that cohousing will become readily accepted as a successful model forcohousing in the U.S. and around the globe.

Thank you for adhering to these criteria when naming your project Cohousing.

Oakcreek Community (left) in Stillwater, OK and Mountain View Community (right) in Mountain View, CA.

About the Authors

Alexandria Levitt is a gerontologist (USC, MS) and community activist based in Southern California. As a gerontologist she is very familiar with the many challenges facing us as we get older and the remarkable connection between health (both mental and physical) and social engagement. In her work with older adults she has seen the toll of social isolation and is concerned that Americans' determination to age in their homes on their own without help from anyone does not serve them well. Though it goes against the "cowboy" in us all, a healthy and happy future is entwined with engagement with others. There are many ways to accomplish this, but Levitt finds cohousing to be the most exciting and progressive example.

Levitt's goal is to create housing in Southern California that doesn't just show off a "lifestyle" imagined by corporate developers but one that reinforces friendship, community, and purpose, as originally envisioned in Denmark's cohousing homes. Such cohousing neighborhoods will be home for active, engaged people (and ideally close to public transit and coffee shops!) and be assets to the neighborhoods that surround them.

Levitt has worked as a nonprofit fundraiser and a documentary filmmaker for PBS. She has served her community in the following ways: a member of the Senior Citizen Commission of South Pasadena, California, a member of the Board of the nonprofit SAGE Senior Cohousing Advocates, a Girl Scout leader for 13 years and a PTA President for 2 years.

Charles Durrett is an architect, author, and advocate of affordable, socially responsible and sustainable design, who has made major contributions to community-based architecture and cohousing. He has designed over fifty cohousing communities in North America and has consulted on many more around the world. He is the principle architect at McCamant and Durrett Architects, based in Nevada City, California. His work has been featured in *Time magazine, New York Times, LA Times, San Francisco Chronicle, Guardian, Architecture, Architectural Record, Wall Street Journal, Economist,* and a wide variety of other publications.

Along with receiving numerous awards for his contribution to cohousing and community-based architecture, he has given many public presentations for groups such as the US Congress, the Commonwealth Club, and scores of universities, city councils and planning commissions around the country. Most importantly, he continues to devote his time to new cohousing groups that are just getting started.

His other works include *Creating Cohousing: Building Sustainable Communities,* the book that introduced cohousing to the United States, and *The Senior Cohousing Handbook: A Community Approach to Independent Living.* He has authored, or co-authored, a half dozen others as well. He lives in Nevada City Cohousing in Northern California, a community he designed in which twenty-one seniors also reside. He previously lived in Doyle Street Cohousing in Emeryville, California, with his family for twelve years. The Oxford English Dictionary credited him, along with partner Katie McCamant, with coining the word *cohousing*.

He realized long ago that developing healthy environments requires starting with the culture–and seeing the much wider array of issues other than the sticks and bricks.

Quimper Village Residents

Half of this book is penned by those that took this journey and then planned to live there together and now do. It was fun to write it with them because they remember the rocks under the water that we bumped into and the trip hazards along the way. It was fun to write with them because of their sometimes-animated recall. And of course, it was fun to write together because of the passion that we share.

Those, in particular, are Carolyn Salmon, David and Pat Hundhausen, Janet Palmer, and all of the good folks we interviewed and queried, including Mack Boelling, Araya Sol, Jerry Spieckerman, Pam Clise, Ivar Dolph, Mena Quilici, and Bill Darlington. Photo credit also belongs to Cheron Dudley, Nancy Richards, Janet Palmer, and the entire QV newsletter team. In reality, the entire group penned their story on their own, at least the outline and then the trajectory itself. That is hard and then easier, but never really done.

250
150 pages
―――
12500

25
15
――
125
25
――
3750 words

{ Atkins
  Mattis -
  Stonecreek sold
  ――――――
  80 Abrev
  ――――
  10 Age

Made in the USA
Coppell, TX
24 April 2020